Summary

After the first Gulf war, in 1991, a new peace process consisting of bilateral negotiations between Israel and the Palestinians, Jordan, Syria, and Lebanon achieved mixed results. Milestones included the Israeli-Palestine Liberation Organization (PLO) Declaration of Principles (DOP) of September 13, 1993, providing for Palestinian empowerment and some territorial control, the Israeli-Jordanian peace treaty of October 26, 1994, and the Interim Self-Rule in the West Bank or Oslo II accord of September 28, 1995, which led to the formation of the Palestinian Authority (PA) to govern the West Bank and Gaza Strip. However, Israeli-Syrian negotiations were intermittent and difficult, and postponed indefinitely in 2000. Israeli-Lebanese negotiations also were unsuccessful, leading Israel to withdraw unilaterally from south Lebanon on May 24, 2000. President Clinton held a summit with Israeli and Palestinian leaders at Camp David on final status issues that July, but they did not produce an accord. A Palestinian uprising or *intifadah* began in September. On February 6, 2001, Ariel Sharon was elected Prime Minister of Israel, and rejected steps taken at Camp David and afterwards.

On April 30, 2003, the United States, the U.N., European Union, and Russia (known as the "Quartet") presented a "Road Map" to Palestinian statehood. It has not been implemented. Israel unilaterally disengaged (withdrew) from the Gaza Strip and four small settlements in the West Bank in August 2005. On January 9, 2005, Mahmud Abbas had become President of the PA. The victory of Hamas, which Israel and the United States consider a terrorist group, in the January 2006 Palestinian parliamentary elections complicated prospects for peace as the United States, Israel, and the Quartet would not deal with a Hamas-led government until it disavowed violence, recognized Israel, and accepted prior Israeli-Palestinian accords. President Abbas's dissolution of the Hamas-led government in response to the June 2007 Hamas forcible takeover of the Gaza Strip led to resumed international contacts with the PA. On November 27, at an international conference in Annapolis, MD, President Bush read a Joint Understanding in which Abbas and Israeli Prime Minister Ehud Olmert agreed to simultaneously resume bilateral negotiations on core issues and implement the Road Map. On May 21, 2008, Israel, Syria, and Turkey announced that Syria and Israel had begun indirect peace talks in Istanbul via Turkish mediators. Later in the year, Israeli and U.S. elections appeared to disrupt negotiations on all tracks and the end of the Israeli-Hamas cease-fire in December and the subsequent outbreak of violence in Gaza led to the official suspension of peace talks. President Obama has affirmed U.S. support for a two-state solution to the Israeli-Palestinian conflict and named former Senator George Mitchell as his Special Envoy for Middle East Peace.

Congress is interested in issues related to Middle East peace because of its oversight role in the conduct of U.S. foreign policy, its support for Israel, and keen constituent interest. It is especially concerned about U.S. financial and other commitments to the parties, and the 111th Congress is engaged in these matters. Congress also has endorsed Jerusalem as the undivided capital of Israel, although U.S. Administrations have consistently maintained that the fate of the city is the subject of final status negotiations. This CRS report will be updated as developments warrant. See also CRS Report R40101, *Israel and Hamas: Conflict in Gaza (2008-2009)* , coordinated by Jim Zanotti, CRS Report RS22768, *Israeli-Palestinian Peace Process: The Annapolis Conference*, by Carol Migdalovitz, CRS Report RL33566, *Lebanon: The Israel-Hamas-Hezbollah Conflict*, by Jeremy M. Sharp et al., and CRS Report RS22967, *U.S. Foreign Aid to the Palestinians*, by Jim Zanotti.

Contents

Figures

Contacts

Most Recent Developments

President Obama and Israeli Prime Minister Benjamin Netanyahu met at the White House on May 18, 2009. Afterwards, the President said, "It is in the interests not only of the Palestinians but also the Israelis, the United States, and the international community to achieve a two-state solution in which Israel and the Palestinians are living side by side in peace and security." He also stated, "The Palestinians are going to have to do a better job of providing the kinds of security assurances that Israelis would need to achieve a two-state solution ... the other Arab states have to be more supportive and be bolder in seeking potential normalization with Israel." The President declared, "Settlements have to be stopped in order for us to move forward," and "the humanitarian situation in Gaza has to be addressed." Prime Minister Netanyahu said that he wanted "to start peace negotiations with the Palestinians immediately and to broaden the circle of peace to include others in the Arab world," but that the Palestinians "will have to recognize Israel as a Jewish state" and "enable Israel to have the means to defend itself." If these conditions are met, then he could envision an "arrangement where Palestinians and Israelis live side by side...." He said that Israel wanted the Palestinians to govern themselves, but he did not endorse the goal of a Palestinian state. The two leaders appeared to differ regarding linkage between the peace process and dealing with Iran. The President asserted that "To the extent that we can make peace ...between the Palestinians and Israelis, then I actually think it strengthens our hands in dealing with a potential Iranian threat," whereas the Prime Minister heard the President say "there isn't a policy of linkage," and that he (the Prime Minister) wanted to move "simultaneously and in parallel on both fronts."[1]

On May 21, Secretary of State Hillary Rodham Clinton told *Al-Jazeera*, "We want to see a stop to settlement construction – additions, natural growth, any kind of settlement activity – that is what the President has called for." Prime Minister Netanyahu's spokesman responded, "normal life" in settlements "must be allowed to continue," using a new phrase instead of natural growth.[2]

On May 21, on the anniversary of the annexation of East Jerusalem in 1967, Prime Minister Netanyahu vowed "United Jerusalem is Israel's capital. Jerusalem was always ours and will always be ours. It will never again be partitioned and divided."[3] The Palestinians consider East Jerusalem to be occupied Palestinian territory and ,according the parameters of the 1990's peace process, the fate of Jerusalem is to be decided in negotiations between Israel and the Palestinians. Israel reportedly is offering to remove 26 unauthorized settlements with an estimated 1,200 settlers, not expropriate Palestinian land, and not give financial incentives to people to live in settlements in return for a cessation in U.S. pressure for a complete settlement freeze and for continued "natural growth" of settlements.[4] However, U.S. officials are said not to be receptive. On June 1, Netanyahu told a Knesset committee that halting construction in settlements would be equal to "freezing life,' and therefore, "unreasonable."[5]

---

[1] Remarks by President Obama and Prime Minister Netanyahu of Israel in press availability, May 18, 2009, accessible via http://www.whitehouse.gov.

[2] Amy Teibel, "Israel Rejects Demand for Halt on Settlements," Associated Press, May 29, 2009.

[3] Mark Lavie, "Netanyahu Takes Hard Line on Jerusalem," *Pittsburgh Post-Gazette*, May 22, 2009.

[4] Herb Keinon, "Israeli, US Officials Huddle in UK over Settlements, Iran," *Jerusalem Post*, May 27, 2009.

[5] Helene Cooper, "Obama Talks of Being 'Honest' with Israel," *New York Times*, June 2, 2009.

President Obama restated his position regarding settlements at his May 28 White House meeting with Palestinian Authority (PA) President Mahmud Abbas. The next day, Abbas said, "There are no preset conditions" for holding negotiations, just obligations under the Road Map.[6]

Some disagreement between Israeli and U.S. officials developed over alleged informal agreements regarding a definition of "settlement freeze" that Israelis claim was reached in May 2003 between Prime Minister Ariel Sharon and then U.S. National Security Council officials Elliott Abrams and Stephen Hadley. Sharon's (and now Netanyahu's) advisor Dov Weissglas says that they defined a settlement freeze as "no new communities were to be built; no Palestinian lands were to be appropriated for settlement purposes; building will not take place beyond existing community outlines; and no 'settlement encouraging' budgets were to be allocated."[7] However, Abrams wrote earlier that the guidelines were discussed, "but never formally adopted."[8] Secretary Clinton said, "We have the negotiating record, that is the official record, that was turned over to the Obama administration by the outgoing Bush administration. There is no memorialization of any informal and oral agreements." If such understandings were reached, she noted, "they did not become part of the official position of the United States government. And there are contrary documents that suggest that they were not to be viewed as in any way contradicting the obligations that Israel undertook pursuant to the Road Map. (See "Significant Agreements and Documents.") And those obligations are clear."[9]

In his June 4, speech in Cairo, President Obama said that "just as Israel's right to exist cannot be denied, neither can Palestine's," referring to the state that U.S. officials usually had defined as a future goal. On settlements, he stated, "The United States does not accept the legitimacy of continued Israeli settlements. This construction violates previous agreements and undermines efforts to achieve peace. It is time for these settlements to stop." The only resolution (to the Israeli-Palestinian conflict) is for the aspirations of both sides to be met through two states, where Israelis and Palestinians each live in peace and security." He declared, "(T)he situation for the Palestinian people is intolerable. America will not turn our backs on the legitimate Palestinian aspiration for dignity, opportunity, and a state of their own." Addressing Hamas directly, the President urged it to accept the Quartet's conditions and recognize prior agreements with Israel, recognize Israel's right to exist, and renounce violence. [10]

In Israel on Jun 9, Senator Mitchell noted the controversy over settlements and said, "These are not disagreements among adversaries. The United States and Israel will remain close allies and friends." He added, "focusing on a single issue ill serves the wider diplomatic process" and expressed his desire "to create conditions for the prompt resumption and early conclusion of negotiations." [11]

---

[6] Interview with Al-Arabiyah Television, May 29, 2009, Open Source Center Document GMP20090529647001.

[7] Ethan Bronner, "Bush Deal over 'Freeze" Splits Israel and Obama," *New York Times*, June 4, 2009.

[8] Elliott Abrams, "The Settlement Freeze Fallacy," *Washington Post*, April 8, 2009.

[9] Glenn Kessler, "Clinton Rejects Israeli Claims of Accord on Settlements," *Washington Post*, June 6, 2009.

[10] http://www.whitehouse.gov/the_press_office/Remarks-by-the President-at-Cairo-University-6-04-09/

[11] Barak Ravid, "U.S. Envoy Assures Israel Policy Rift Won't Break Alliance," http://www.haaretz.com, June 9, 2009.

Background

Before the first Gulf war in 1991, Arab-Israeli conflict marked every decade since the founding of Israel. With each clash, issues separating the parties multiplied and became more intractable. The creation of the State of Israel in 1948 provided a home for the Jewish people, but the ensuing conflict made refugees of hundreds of thousands of Arab residents of formerly British Palestine, with consequences troubling for Arabs and Israelis alike. It also led to a mass movement of Jewish citizens of Arab states to Israel. The 1967 war ended with Israel occupying territory of Egypt, Jordan, and Syria. Egypt and Syria fought the 1973 war, in part, to regain their lands. In 1982, Israel invaded southern Lebanon to prevent terrorist incursions; it withdrew in 1985, but retained a 9-mile "security zone" that Lebanon sought to reclaim. Middle East peace has been a U.S. and international diplomatic goal throughout the years of conflict. The 1978 Camp David talks, the only previous direct Arab-Israeli negotiations, brought about the 1979 Israel-Egypt Peace Treaty.[12]

U.S. Role

1991-2008

At the beginning of the Gulf war in 1991, President George H.W. Bush declared solving the Arab-Israeli conflict among his postwar goals. On March 6, 1991, he outlined a framework for peace based on U.N. Security Council Resolutions 242 and 338 and the principle of "land for peace." Secretary of State James Baker organized a peace conference in Madrid in October 1991 that launched almost a decade of the "Oslo process" to achieve peace. It continued under President William Clinton, who asserted that only the region's leaders can make peace and vowed to be their partner. With the Hebron Protocol of 1997, however, the United States seemed to become an indispensable and expected party to Israeli-Palestinian talks. Clinton mediated the 1998 Wye River Memorandum, and the United States coordinated its implementation. He personally led negotiations at Camp David in 2000.

The George W. Bush administration initially sought a less prominent role, and Secretary of State Colin Powell did not appoint a special Middle East envoy. After the September 11, 2001, terrorist attacks, the Administration focused on the peace process mainly as part of the war on terrorism. Secretary of State Condoleezza Rice also did not name a special envoy, asserting, "Not every effort has to be an American effort. It is extremely important that the parties themselves are taking responsibility."[13] She encouraged Israelis and Palestinians to act, but personally mediated a November 2005 accord to reopen the border crossing between Gaza and Egypt after Israel's withdrawal from Gaza. In 2007, she engaged again partly in order to elicit the support of moderate Sunni Arab governments to thwart the rise of Iranian influence. Those governments see

---

[12] For additional background, see William B. Quandt, *Peace Process, American Diplomacy and the Arab-Israeli Conflict since 1967*, Washington, DC, Brookings Institution Press, Revised Edition 2001; Charles Enderlin, *Shattered Dreams: The Failure of the Peace Process in the Middle East*, New York, Other Press, 2003; Anton La Guardia, *War Without End: Israelis Palestinians and the Struggle for a Promised Land*, New York, St. Martin's Griffin, Revised and Updated, 2003; Alan Dowty, *Israel/Palestine*, Cambridge, UK, Polity Press, 2005; and Dennis Ross, *The Missing Peace: The Inside Story of the Fight for Middle East Peace*, New York, Farrar, Straus and Giroux, 2004.

[13] Anne Gearan, "Rice Blasts Way Iran Treats Its Own People," Associated Press, February 4, 2005.

---

resolution of the Palestinian issue as a key to regional stability and to denying Iran opportunities for destabilizing actions.

The Joint Understanding presented at the November 2007 Annapolis Conference created a new role for the United States as "judge" of Israel's and the Palestinians' fulfillment of their commitments under the 2003 international Road Map to a two-state solution. In January 2008, President Bush appointed (Air Force) Lt. Gen. William Fraser III, assistant to the Chairman of the Joint Chiefs of Staff, to monitor the parties' compliance with their commitments. Gen. Fraser , who has been replaced by Lt. Gen. Paul J. Selva, was not to mediate or enforce compliance. Instead, according to National Security Advisor Stephen Hadley, Fraser "will be in dialogue with Palestinians and Israelis and get the facts on what each of them is doing to implement the Road Map—what they are doing, what they are not doing—and to bring that to their attention ... encouraging the parties to move forward on their obligations to complete the Road Map."[14] Fraser was to visit the region "from time to time," but the trilateral mechanism barely functioned.

Obama Administration

At her January 13, 2009, Senate confirmation hearing, Secretary of State-designate Hillary Rodham Clinton, said that the Gaza conflict "must only increase our determination to seek a just and lasting peace agreement that brings real security to Israel—normal and positive relations with its neighbors, independence, economic progress, and security to the Palestinians in their own state. We will exert every effort to support the work of Israelis and Palestinians who seek that result...." She added that the United States would not negotiate with Hamas until it recognizes Israel, renounces violence, and abides by previous agreements. "That is just an absolute for me. That is the United States' position and the president-elect's position."

On his first full day in office, January 21, President Obama telephoned Palestinian Authority (PA) President Abbas, Israeli Prime Minister Olmert, Egyptian President Hosni Mubarak, and Jordanian King Abdullah II "to communicate his commitment to active engagement in pursuit of Arab-Israeli peace from the beginning of his term." The next day, the President and Secretary Clinton jointly announced the appointment of former Senator George Mitchell as their Special Envoy for Middle East Peace. The President emphasized that Mitchell was "fully empowered" to speak for the White House and State Department, thereby boosting his emissary's clout.

On January 27, President Obama gave his first television interview to *Al Arabiyah* television. He said, "I think it is possible for us to see a Palestinian state—I am not going to put a timeframe on it—that is contiguous, that allows freedom of movement for its people, that allows for trade with other countries, that allows the creation of businesses and commerce so that people have a better life."

During his first trip to the region, Senator Mitchell visited Israel, the West Bank, Jordan, Egypt, and Saudi Arabia, but not the Gaza Strip or Syria. His goals were to listen to the region's leaders' views on an Israeli-Palestinian settlement, to try to stabilize the unofficial cease-fire in Gaza, and to ensure that humanitarian aid is delivered swiftly to Gaza's needy. On January 29, Mitchell said, "Lasting peace is our objective. The United States will sustain an active commitment to two sides living side by side in peace, stability, and security."

---

[14] Press Briefing, January 10, 2008, http://georgewbush-whitehouse.archives.gov/news/releases/2008/01/20080110-7 html.

Mitchell reportedly told Prime Minister Olmert that the Obama Administration stands behind the commitments in an April 2004 letter that President Bush gave to then Prime Minister Ariel Sharon.[15] In a conference call with Jewish leaders on February 19, Mitchell is said to have expressed support for Egyptian efforts to forge a Palestinian unity government with Fatah and Hamas because divisions among the Palestinians have been an obstacle to bringing peace to the region. He said that Hamas still would need to fulfill the demands that it halt violence, recognize Israel, and accept previous Israeli-Palestinian agreements, and that the chances of Hamas doing that were not good.[16] Mitchell returned to the region on February 26, when he met Israeli Prime Minister-designate Benjamin Netanyahu and others.

On March 2, Secretary Clinton told an international donors conference in Sharm al Shaykh that "The United States is committed to a comprehensive peace between Israel and its Arab neighbors, and we will pursue it on many fronts." She announced more than $900 million in aid for the Palestinians and stated that there are safeguards to ensure that no funds go to Hamas. The funds include $300 million in humanitarian aid for Gaza and $600 million in budget and development aid for the Palestinian Authority. (For more on this aid package, see CRS Report RS22967, *U.S. Foreign Aid to the Palestinians*, by Jim Zanotti.)

In Israel on March 3, the Secretary expressed understanding of Israel's need not "to stand idly by while its territory and people are subjected to rocket attacks." The next day, in Ramallah, Clinton described Israel's plans to demolish 88 Palestinian homes in East Jerusalem as "unhelpful and not in keeping with the obligations entered into under the Road Map," and with far-reaching implications.[17] She said that the issue would be raised with the new Israeli government and the municipal government in Jerusalem. Throughout, Secretary Clinton emphasized the Obama Administration's commitment to the two-state solution, saying that it was in Israel's best interests.

Senator Mitchell made his third trip to the region in mid-April. The Israeli Government Press Office said that the Prime Minister told him that it will not be possible to advance the diplomatic process and reach a peace settlement without recognition of Israel as the national state of the Jewish People. However, Netanyahu did not set this as a precondition for opening negotiations with the Palestinians.[18] Mitchell said that U.S. policy on a two-state solution "would have a Palestinian state living in peace along the Jewish state of Israel."[19] Palestinians contend that recognition of Israel as a Jewish state would negate Palestinian refugee's "right of return" and would be detrimental to the status of Israel's Arab citizens. On April 27, Palestinian Authority (PA) President Abbas said, "Its not my job to give a description to the state. Name yourself the Hebrew Socialist Republic—it is none of my business."[20] According to his spokesman, in his meeting with Mitchell, President Abbas stressed the commitment of the Palestinians to a two-state solution and signed agreements and obligations, particularly freezing settlement activities, including natural growth, stopping house demolitions, and not building in E-1 (a corridor of land between Israel and the Ma'ale Adumim West Bank settlement), and demanded that the same

---

[15] Ibid. For text of letters, see Israel's Ministry of Foreign Affairs at http://www.mfa.gov.il/MFA/Peace+Process/ Reference+Documents/Exchange+of+letters+Sharon-Bush+14-Apr-2004.htm.

[16] Hilary Leila Krieger, "Mitchell could Support PA Unity Gov't," *Jerusalem Post*, February 19, 2009.

[17] Paul Richter, "In West Bank, Clinton Criticizes Israel," *Los Angeles Times*, March 5, 2009.

[18] "Netanyahu Drops Demand for Jewish State Recognition," Open Source Center Summary, April 20, 2009, Document GMP20090420738011.

[19] Isabel Kershner, "Israel: Netanyahu Demands Recognition of Israel First," *New York Times*, April 17, 2009.

[20] Isabel Kershner, "Abbas Rejects Calling Israel a Jewish State," *New York Times*, April 28, 2009.

criteria be applied to Israel.[21] Mitchell spoke again about the U.S. commitment to an independent Palestinian state, and said that the United States wanted the Arab Peace Initiative to be part of the effort to reach this goal.

On April 22, after meeting King Abdullah II of Jordan, President Obama said that he had invited the leaders of Israel, Egypt, and the Palestinians to the White House for separate talks over the following six weeks. The President expressed hope that "over the next several months that you start seeing gestures of good faith on all sides.... I think that the parties in the region probably have a pretty good recognition of what intermediate steps could be taken as confidence-building measures. And we will be doing everything we can to encourage" those measures. The President described a U.S. role as helping to "create the conditions and the atmosphere and provide the help and assistance that facilitate an agreement."[22]

On April 23, Secretary Clinton told the House Appropriations Committee Subcommittee on State, Foreign Operations, and Related Programs that "for Israel to get the kind of strong support it is looking for vis-à-vis Iran, it can't stay on the sidelines with respect to the Palestinians and the peace efforts. They go hand in hand." She added that the Arab governments "believe that Israel's willingness to reenter into discussions with the Palestinian Authority strengthens them in being able to deal with Iran." On April 30, the Secretary told the Senate Appropriations Committee that reports of U.S. funding for a Palestinian government that includes Hamas are wrong. She said for a Palestinian unity government to receive U.S. funding, "the government itself plus every member of the government would have to commit to the Quartet's principles."

In a speech to AIPAC on May 5, Vice President Joe Biden called on Israel to work toward a two-state solution, not build more settlements, dismantle outposts, and allow the Palestinians freedom of movement. Chairman of the Senate Foreign Relations Committee John Kerry told the same gathering that settlements "don't just fragment a future Palestinian state. They also fragment what the Israeli Defense Forces must defend, they undercut Abbas, and strengthen Hamas by convincing the Palestinians that there is no reward for moderation." He warned that the "window of opportunity is fast closing."

Madrid Conference

The peace conference opened on October 30, 1991. Parties were represented by 14-member delegations. A combined Jordanian/Palestinian delegation had 14 representatives from each. An unofficial Palestinian advisory team coordinated with the Palestine Liberation Organization (PLO). The United States, the Soviet Union, Syria, Palestinians/Jordan, the European Community, Egypt, Israel, and Lebanon sat at the table. The U.N., the Gulf Cooperation Council,[23] and the Arab Maghreb Union[24] were observers.

---

[21] "PLO Negotiator Holds Joint Conference with US Envoy Mitchell in West Bank," Palestinian News Agency Wafa, April 17, 2009, BBC Monitoring Middle East, April 18, 2009.

[22] Paul Richter, "Obama Gets Ball Rolling on Mideast," *Los Angeles Times*, April 22, 2009.

[23] The Gulf Cooperation Council is comprised of Bahrain, Kuwait, Oman, Qatar, Saudi Arabia, and the United Arab Emirates.

[24] The Arab Maghreb Union is comprised of Algeria, Libya, Mauritania, Morocco, and Tunisia.

Bilateral Talks and Developments

Israel-Palestinians

At End of Israeli Prime Minister Barak's Tenure

(Incidents of violence are noted selectively.) In November 1991, Israel and the Jordanian/Palestinian delegation agreed to separate Israeli-Jordanian and Israeli-Palestinian negotiating tracks, the latter to address a five-year period of interim Palestinian self-rule in the West Bank and Gaza Strip. In the third year, permanent status negotiations were to begin. On August 9, 1993, Palestinian negotiators were appointed to a PLO coordination committee, ending efforts to make it appear that the PLO was not part of the talks. Secret talks in Oslo, Norway produced a Declaration of Principles (DOP), signed by Israel and the PLO on September 13, 1993. Through the end of the decade, incremental advances were made, including Israel's withdrawal from major cities and towns and Palestinian self-government as the Palestinian Authority (PA). However, no final agreement was reached. (See "Significant Agreements," below, for summaries of and links to accords reached between 1993 and 2000. This narrative resumes with the Camp David summit.)

President Clinton, Israeli Prime Minister Ehud Barak, and PA Chairman Yasir Arafat held a summit at Camp David, from July 11 to July 24, 2000, to forge a framework accord on final status issues. They did not succeed. The parties had agreed that there would be no agreement unless all issues were resolved. Jerusalem was the major obstacle. Israel proposed that it remain united under its sovereignty, leaving the Palestinians control, not sovereignty, over East Jerusalem and Muslim holy sites. Israel was willing to cede more than 90% of the West Bank, wanted to annex settlements where about 130,000 settlers lived, and offered to admit thousands of Palestinian refugees in a family unification program. An international fund would compensate other refugees as well as Israelis from Arab countries. The Palestinians reportedly were willing to accept Israeli control over the Jewish quarter of Jerusalem and the Western Wall, but sought sovereignty over East Jerusalem, particularly the Haram al Sharif/Temple Mount, a site holy to Jews and Muslims.

On September 28, Israeli opposition leader Ariel Sharon, with 1,000 security forces, visited the Temple Mount/Haram al Sharif. Palestinians protested, and Israel responded forcefully. The second Palestinian *intifadah* or uprising against the Israeli occupation began as a mob in Ramallah killed two Israeli soldiers, provoking Israeli helicopter gunship attacks on Palestinian official sites on October 12.

Barak resigned on December 10, triggering an early election for Prime Minister in Israel. Further negotiations were held at Bolling Air Force Base, in Washington, D.C., December 19-23. On December 23, President Clinton suggested that Israel cede sovereignty over the Temple Mount/Haram al Sharif and Arab neighborhoods in Jerusalem, 96% of the West Bank, all of the Gaza Strip, and annex settlement blocs in exchange for giving the Palestinians Israeli land near Gaza. Jerusalem would be the capital of two countries. The Palestinians would cede the right of refugees to return to Israel and accept a Jewish "connection" to the Temple Mount and sovereignty over the Western Wall and holy sites beneath it. The agreement would declare "an end to conflict."[25] Barak said he would accept the plan as a basis for further talks if Arafat did so. Arafat sought clarifications on contiguity of Palestinian state territory, the division of East Jerusalem, and refugees' right of return, among other issues. The Israeli-Palestinian talks concluded at Taba, Egypt.

Sharon

On February 6, 2001, Ariel Sharon was elected Prime Minister of Israel and vowed to retain united Jerusalem as Israel's capital, the Jordan Valley, and other areas for security. Sharon's associates asserted that the results of negotiations at and after Camp David were "null and void."[26] The Bush Administration said that Clinton's proposals were no longer U.S. proposals.[27] Sharon sought an interim agreement, not dealing with Jerusalem, Palestinian refugees, or a Palestinian state and, in an interview published on April 13, said that he could accept a disarmed Palestinian state on 42% of the West Bank.[28]

On September 24, Sharon declared, "Israel wants to give the Palestinians what no one else gave them before, the possibility of a state." On October 2, President Bush said, for the first time, "The idea of a Palestinian state has always been part of a vision, so long as the right of Israel to exist is respected."[29] On November 10, he declared that the United States is "working toward the day when two states—Israel and Palestine—live peacefully together within secure and recognized borders...."

Secretary Powell sent General Anthony Zinni, USMC (Ret.) to work on a cease-fire, but violence impeded his mission. Israel confined Arafat to his headquarters in Ramallah on December 3. On December 7, Sharon doubted that an accord could be reached with Arafat, "who is a real terrorist."[30] On December 12, Hamas ambushed an Israeli bus in the West Bank and perpetrated two simultaneous suicide bombings in Gaza. The Israeli cabinet charged that Arafat was "directly responsible" for the attacks "and therefore is no longer relevant."[31]

On January 3, 2002, Israeli forces seized the Karine A, a Palestinian-commanded freighter, carrying 50 tons of Iranian-supplied arms. Secretary Powell stated that Arafat "cannot engage with us and others in the pursuit of peace, and at the same time permit or tolerate continued violence and terror." At the White House on February 7, Sharon said that he believed that pressure should be put on Arafat so that an alternative Palestinian leadership could emerge.

---

[25] For text of the President's speech describing his proposal, also known as "the Clinton Plan" or "Clinton Parameters," see the Israel Policy Forum website at http://www.israelpolicyforum.org/display.cfm?rid=544.

[26] Lee Hockstader, "Jerusalem is 'Indivisible,' Sharon Says; Camp David Concessions are Called 'Null and Void,'" *Washington Post*, February 8, 2001.

[27] Jane Perlez, "Bush Officials Pronounce Clinton Mideast Plan Dead," *New York Times*, February 9, 2001.

[28] Interview by Ari Shavit, *Haaretz*, April 13, 2001, Foreign Broadcast Information Service (FBIS) Document GMP20011041300070.

[29] See http://georgewbush-whitehouse.archives.gov.

[30] *Newsweek* interview, quoted by Ibrahim Barzak, "Jewish Settlements Mortared in Gaza; Israel Leader Raps Arafat in Interview, Associated Press, December 9, 2001.

[31] "Israeli Cabinet Decision on Cutting Contacts with Arafat," Government Press Office, December 13, 2001, FBIS Document GMP20011121300010.

On February 17, Saudi Crown Prince (later King) Abdullah unprecedentedly called for "full withdrawal from all occupied territories, in accord with U.N. resolutions, including Jerusalem, in exchange for full normalization of relations." On March 28, the Arab League endorsed his proposal with some revisions; it is known as the "Arab Peace Initiative."[32] Prime Minister Sharon said that he was willing to explore the idea but that it would be a "mistake" to replace U.N. resolutions affirming Israel's right to "secure and recognized borders" with total withdrawal to pre-1967 borders.

On March 27, Hamas perpetrated a suicide bombing at a hotel in Netanya during Passover celebrations, killing 27 and wounding 130. Israel declared Arafat "an enemy" and Israeli forces besieged his compound in Ramallah; they soon controlled all major Palestinian-ruled West Bank cities.

On June 24, President Bush called on the Palestinians to elect new leaders "not compromised by terror" and to build a practicing democracy. Then, he said, the United States will support the creation of a Palestinian state, whose borders and certain aspects of sovereignty will be provisional until a final settlement. He added, "as we make progress toward security, Israeli forces need to withdraw fully to positions they held prior to September 28, 2000 ... and (Israeli) settlement activity must stop." The President foresaw a final peace accord within three years.[33] On September 17, the Quartet (U.S., European Union (EU), U.N., and Russian officials) outlined a preliminary "Road Map" to peace based on the President's ideas. (See "Significant Agreements," below for summary and link.)

On March 7, 2003, in what was seen as a gesture to appeal to the Quartet, Arafat named Mahmud Abbas (aka Abu Mazen) Prime Minister. On April 14, Prime Minister Sharon acknowledged that Israel would have to part with some places bound up in the history of the Jewish people, but insisted that the Palestinians recognize the Jewish people's right to its homeland and abandon their claim of a right of refugees to return to Israel.[34] Also on April 14, Israel submitted 14 reservations on the Road Map.[35] On April 30, the Quartet officially presented the Road Map. Abbas accepted it. On May 23, the Bush Administration stated that Israel had explained its concerns and that the United States shares the view "that these are real concerns and will address them fully and seriously in the implementation of the Road Map," leading Sharon and his cabinet to accept "steps defined" in the Road Map "with reservations" on May 25. The next day, Sharon declared, "to keep 3.5 million people under occupation is bad for us and them," using the word occupation for the first time.

On June 4, President Bush met Abbas and Sharon in Aqaba, Jordan. Abbas vowed to achieve the Palestinians' goals by peaceful means, while Sharon expressed understanding of "the importance of territorial contiguity" for a viable Palestinian state and promised to "remove unauthorized outposts" in the West Bank. Abbas said that he would use dialogue, not force, to convince Palestinian groups. On June 29, Hamas and Palestine Islamic Jihad (PIJ) suspended military operations against Israel for three months, while Fatah declared a six-month truce. Israel was not

---

[32] For "Arab Peace Initiative," see http://www.al-bab.com/arab/docs/league/peace02.htm.

[33] For text of the speech, see http://geogewbush-whtehouse.archives.gov/news/releases/2002/06/20020624-3 html.

[34] "Sharon, 'Certain' of Passing 'Painful Concessions' in Knesset," *Ma'ariv*, April 15, 2003, FBIS Document GMP20030415000091.

[35] For text of Israel's reservations, see Israel's Response to the Road Map, online at http://www.knesset.gov.il/process/docs/Road Map_response_eng.htm.

a party to the accord, but began withdrawing forces from Gaza. Abbas asked Sharon to release Palestinian prisoners, remove roadblocks, withdraw from more Palestinian cities, allow Arafat free movement, and end construction of a security barrier that Israeli is building in the West Bank. Israel demanded that the Palestinians dismantle terrorist infrastructures and act against terrorists. Neither fulfilled the other's request.

On August 6, Israel released 339 prisoners. On August 19, a Hamas suicide bomber exploded in Jerusalem, killing 22, including 5 Americans, and injuring more than 130. Abbas cut contacts with Hamas and the PIJ, and unsuccessfully sought Arafat's support to act against terrorists. Israel suspended talks with the Palestinians, halted plans to transfer cities to their control, and resumed "targeted killings" of terrorist leaders, among other measures. On September 6, Abbas resigned because of what he charged was lack of support from Arafat, the United States, and Israel.

On October 15, a bomb detonated under an official U.S. vehicle in Gaza, killing three U.S. security guards and wounding a fourth. Palestinian authorities arrested members of Popular Resistance Committees, who would be freed in April 2004.

Sounds of discontent with government policy were heard in Israel, culminating in the signing of the Geneva Accord, a Draft Permanent Status Agreement by Israeli opposition politicians and prominent Palestinians on December 1.[36] Perhaps partly to defuse these efforts, on December 18, Sharon declared that, "to ensure a Jewish and democratic Israel," he would unilaterally disengage from the Palestinians by redeploying Israeli forces and relocating settlements in the Gaza Strip and intensifying construction of the security fence in the West Bank.[37] On February 13, 2004, the White House said that an Israeli pullback "could reduce friction," but that a final settlement "must be achieved through negotiations." After an upsurge in violence, Israeli missiles killed Hamas leader Shaykh Ahmed Yassin on March 22.

On April 14, President Bush and Sharon met and exchanged letters.[38] The President welcomed Israel's plan to disengage from Gaza and restated the U.S. commitment to the Road Map. He noted the need to take into account changed "realities on the ground, including already existing major Israeli population centers," (i.e., settlements), asserting "it is unrealistic to expect that the outcome of final status negotiations will be full and complete return to the armistice lines of 1949." The President stated that a solution to the refugee issue will be found by settling Palestinian refugees in a Palestinian state, "rather than in Israel," thereby rejecting a "right of return." He called for a Palestinian state that is "viable, contiguous, sovereign, and independent." Sharon presented his disengagement plan as independent of but "not inconsistent with the Road Map." He said that the "temporary" security fence that Israel is constructing in the West Bank would not prejudice final status issues including borders. A day before, he had identified five large West Bank settlements and an area in Hebron that Israel intends to retain and strengthen. Palestinians denounced the President's "legitimization" of settlements and prejudgment of final status. On April 18, Sharon's chief of staff Dov Weissglas gave National Security Adviser

---

[36] For text, see the Geneva Initiative website at http://www.heskem.org.il.

[37] For text, see "Sharon Outlines Disengagement Plan from Palestinians in Herzliyya Speech," Parts 1 and 2, Voice of Israel, December 18, 2003, Open Source Center Documents GMP20031218000215 and GMP200312180002167.

[38] For text of letters, see Israel's Ministry of Foreign Affairs at http://www.mfa.gov.il/MFA/Peace+Process/ Reference+Documents/Exchange+of+letters+Sharon-Bush+14-Apr-2004 htm.

Condoleezza Rice a written commitment to dismantle settlement outposts that Israel itself considers illegal.[39] Israel has not fulfilled this commitment.

On June 6, Israel's cabinet approved a compromise disengagement plan whereby Israel would evacuate all 21 settlements in the Gaza Strip and 4 settlements in the northern West Bank. On June 30, the Israeli High Court of Justice upheld the government's right to build a security fence in the West Bank, but struck down some land confiscation orders for violating Palestinian rights and ordered the route to be changed. In subsequent rulings, the Israeli Court has attempted to balance Israel's security needs and the humanitarian claims of Palestinians and has sometimes required that the barrier be rerouted. On July 9, the International Court of Justice (ICJ) issued a non-binding, advisory opinion that the wall violates international law.[40]

On October 6, Weissglas claimed that disengagement was aimed at freezing the political process in order to "prevent the establishment of a Palestinian state and a debate regarding refugees, borders, and Jerusalem."[41]

Yasir Arafat died on November 11. Mahmud Abbas became Chairman of the PLO and, on January 9, 2005, was elected President of the PA. He called for implementing the Road Map while beginning discussion of final status issues and cautioned against interim solutions to delay reaching a comprehensive solution.

Secretary Rice visited Israel and the PA on February 7. She praised the Israelis' "historic" disengagement decision, discussed the need to carry out obligations concerning settlements and outposts, and warned them not to undermine Abbas. She appointed Lt. Gen. William Ward as Middle East Security Coordinator and emphasized the importance of Israeli-Palestinian security cooperation for the disengagement. (Lt. Gen. Keith W. Dayton succeeded Ward in November 2005.)

On February 20, Israel's cabinet adopted a revised route for the security fence closer to the pre-1967 border in some areas, taking about 7% to 8% of the West Bank that includes major settlement blocs. On March 20, it was reported that Israel's defense minister had approved the building of 3,500 new housing units between the Ma'ale Adumim settlement and East Jerusalem, in the E-1 corridor. Critics charge that the construction would cut East Jerusalem off from Palestinian territory, impose a barrier between the northern and southern West Bank, and prevent a future contiguous Palestinian state. Secretary Rice asserted that the plan was "at odds with American policy." On April 11, President Bush conveyed to Sharon his "concern that Israel not undertake any activity that contravenes Road Map obligations or prejudices final status negotiations." Sharon responded, "It is the position of Israel that the major Israeli population centers will remain in Israel's hands under any final status agreement," declared that Ma'ale Adumim is a major population center, and, therefore, Israel is interested in contiguity between it and Jerusalem.

---

[39] For text, see http://www.mfa.gov.il/MFA/Peace+Process/Reference+Documents/Letter+Weissglas-Rice+18-Apr-2004 htm.

[40] For text, see http://www.icj-cij.org. Note, Israel refers to the barrier as a "fence" and the Palestinians and other critics refer to it as a "wall." Neutral observers often use the word "barrier."

[41] Interview by Ari Shavit, "The Big Freeze," *Haaretz*, October 8, 2004, FBIS Document GMP20041008000026.

On May 26, President Bush met Abbas and said that "changes to the 1949 armistice lines must be mutually agreed to." Bush reaffirmed, "A viable two-state solution must ensure contiguity of the West Bank, and a state of scattered territories will not work. There must also be meaningful linkages between the West Bank and Gaza. This is the position of the United States today, it will be the position of the United States at the time of final status negotiations." He also said, "The barrier being erected by Israel ... must be a security, rather than political, barrier." Abbas stated that the boundaries of a future state should be those of before the 1967 war and that "there is no justification for the wall and it is illegitimate."

Palestine Islamic Jihad (PIJ) claimed responsibility for a suicide bombing in Netanya on July 12, killing 5 and injuring more than 90. Meanwhile, Hamas increased rocket and mortar fire against settlements in Gaza and towns in southern Israel in order to show that disengagement meant that Hamas was forcing Israel to withdraw from the Strip.

On August 15, Defense Minister Shaul Mofaz said that Israel would keep the settlement blocs of Ma'ale Adumim, the Etzyon Bloc, Efrat, Ari'el, Qedumim-Qarney Shomrom, and Rehan Shaqed—all are within or expected to be on Israel's side of the security barrier. Mofaz added that Israel would retain the Jordan Rift Valley to guarantee Israel's eastern border.[42]

Israel evacuated all settlements in the Gaza Strip and four small settlements in the northern West Bank between August 17 and August 23. On August 29, Sharon declared that there would be no further disengagements and that the next step must be negotiations under the Road Map. He noted that while large settlement blocs would remain in Israeli hands and linked territorially to Israel, not all West Bank settlements would remain, This would be decided in the final stage of negotiations.

On September 27, Hamas claimed responsibility for kidnapping and killing an Israeli settler in the West Bank. Israel responded with air and artillery strikes, closure of charities linked to terror groups, mass arrests including likely Hamas candidates in Palestinian parliamentary elections, and targeted killings of terrorists. On October 20, President Bush pressed Abbas to "confront the threat armed gangs pose to a genuinely democratic Palestine," but did not urge him to prevent Hamas from participating in parliamentary elections or to request that candidates renounce violence. Abbas said that they would be asked to renounce violence after election.

On October 26, a PIJ suicide bomber killed 6 and wounded more than 20 in Hadera, on the Israeli coast. Sharon announced an offensive against terrorism. He ruled out talks with Abbas until Abbas takes "serious action" against armed groups.

On November 14-15, Secretary Rice visited Israel and the PA. Sharon told her that Israel would not interfere if Hamas participated in the January 2006 Palestinian legislative elections, but warned that if an armed terrorist organization is a partner in the Palestinian administration it could lead to the end of the Road Map. Rice asserted that it would be easier to compel Hamas to disarm after the elections because the entire international community would then exert pressure. Rice vowed not to have contacts with an armed Hamas even if it were part of the Palestinian administration.[43] On November 15, she announced that Israel and the PA had reached an

---

[42] Interview by Golan Yokhpaz, IDF Radio, August 15, 2005, FBIS Document GMP20050815621002.
[43] "Israel: 'Sharp' Sharon-Rice 'Dispute" over Hamas Election Participation Reported, " *Haaretz*, November 14, 2005, Open Source Center Document GMP20051114614002.

Agreement on Movement and Access from the Gaza Strip. After PIJ perpetrated another suicide bombing in Netanya on December 5, Israel did not hold scheduled talks with the PA about West Bank-Gaza bus convoys foreseen in the November 15 agreement.

After Hamas's victories in December 2005 Palestinian municipal elections, speculation increased about possible effects on the peace process if Hamas were similarly successful in January 25, 2006, parliamentary elections. On December 28, the Quartet stated that a future Palestinian cabinet "should include no member who has not committed to the principles of Israel's right to exist in peace and security and an unequivocal end to violence and terrorism."[44] On January 11, 2006, Secretary Rice declared, "It remains the view of the United States that there should be no place in the political process for groups or individuals who refuse to renounce terror and violence, recognize Israel's right to exist, and disarm."

Olmert

On January 4, 2006, Prime Minister Sharon suffered an incapacitating stroke and Deputy Prime Minister Ehud Olmert became Acting Prime Minister. On January 12, Olmert told President Bush that peace efforts could not progress if Hamas joined the Palestinian government.

Hamas won the January 25 Palestinian parliamentary elections. It is a U.S.-designated Foreign Terrorist Organization (FTO), claims the entire land of Palestine, including Israel, "from the [Jordan] river to the [Mediterranean] sea" as an Islamic trust, rejects the Oslo agreements of the 1990s, insists on the right of Palestinian refugees to return to Israel, and on the right to "resistance," which it claims forced Israel from the Gaza Strip.[45] Olmert declared that Israel would not negotiate with a Palestinian administration that included an armed terrorist organization calling for its destruction and demanded that Hamas disarm, annul its Covenant that calls for the destruction of Israel, and accept all prior agreements. President Bush stated that the United States would not deal with a political party "that articulates the destruction of Israel as part of its platform."

On January 30, the Quartet stated that "future assistance to any new (Palestinian) government would be reviewed by donors against the government's commitment to the principles of non-violence, recognition of Israel, and acceptance of previous agreements and obligations, including the Road Map."[46] Hamas countered that it would never recognize Israel, would consider negotiating a "long-term truce" if Israel withdrew to its 1967 borders, released all prisoners, destroyed all settlements, and recognized the Palestinian refugees' right to return (to Israel), and would create a state on "any inch" of Palestinian territory without ceding another.

On February 8, Olmert said that Israel was moving toward a separation from the Palestinians and permanent borders that would include a united Jerusalem, major settlement blocs, and the Jordan Valley. Palestinian Prime Minister-designate Ismail Haniyah of Hamas declared, "Let them withdraw. We will make the Authority stronger on every inch of liberated land...." Damascus-based Hamas Political Bureau Chairman Khalid Mish'al said that his group would make no concessions and would "practice resistance side by side with politics as long as the occupation continued."

---

[44] This and subsequent Quartet statements cited may be found at http://2001-2009.state.gov.

[45] For Hamas Covenant text, see http://www.yale.edu/lawweb/avalon/mideast/hamas htm.

[46] "UN: Statement by Middle East Quartet," M2 Presswire, January 31, 2006.

After his Kadima party placed first in the March 28 Israeli parliamentary elections, Olmert said that he aspired to demarcate permanent borders for a Jewish state with a permanent Jewish majority and a democracy. He called for negotiations based on mutual recognition, agreements already signed, the principles of the Road Map, a halt to violence, and the disarming of terrorist organizations. Haniyah said that Hamas would not object to Abbas negotiating with Israel. In an op-ed in (the British newspaper) *The Guardian* on March 31, Haniyah appealed for no more talk about recognizing Israel's "right to exist" or ending resistance until Israel commits to withdraw from the Palestinians' lands and recognizes their rights.

On April 9, the Israeli security cabinet recommended severing all ties with the Hamas-led PA, which it called a "hostile entity." Because it viewed the PA as "one authority and not as having two heads," the cabinet declared that there could be personal contacts, but not negotiations, with President Abbas. On April 17, PIJ carried out a suicide bombing in Tel Aviv, killing 11 and wounding 60, including an American teenager. Abbas condemned the attack as "despicable" and counter to Palestinian interests, while Hamas officials called it an act of "self-defense."

On April 26, Abbas called for an immediate international peace conference with himself as the Palestinian negotiator. He claimed that the Hamas-led government was not an obstacle to negotiations because the PLO, which he heads, had the mandate to negotiate as it had all previous agreements. He noted that he was empowered as the democratically elected leader of the Palestinians.

On May 4, a new Israeli government took office, with guidelines vowing to strive to shape the permanent borders of the State of Israel as a democratic state, with a Jewish majority. Prime Minister Olmert asserted that the security fence would be adapted to conform to borders. The PLO rejected the Olmert plan as aimed at undermining the Palestinian people's right to a state on all territories occupied in 1967, with Jerusalem as its capital.

On May 10, imprisoned Fatah, Hamas, and other officials drafted a "National Accord Document" calling for a Palestinian state with Jerusalem as its capital, the right of the return of refugees, and the release of all prisoners. It also called for renewing the PLO and for Hamas and PIJ to join it, supported the right to resist the occupation in lands occupied in 1967, and stated that the PLO is responsible for negotiations and that any agreement should be put to a vote by the Palestinian National Council or a referendum.[47] Abbas accepted the document, but Hamas rejected its implied recognition of pre-1967 Israel.

On May 23, at the White House, President Bush accepted that Olmert's ideas for removing Israeli settlements could lead to a two-state solution if a pathway to progress on the Road Map is not open in the period ahead. Olmert said that he had presented ideas for a "realignment" in the West Bank to "reduce friction between Israelis and Palestinians, ensure territorial contiguity for the Palestinians, and guarantee Israel's security as a Jewish state with the borders it desires."[48]

Violence increased between Gaza and Israel. The Hamas military wing and other groups repeatedly launched rockets at Sderot in southern Israel, and Israel responded with artillery fire

---

[47] For text of a later, final version of the National Accord Document (also known as the Palestinian Prisoners's Agreement), see Palestine Liberation Organization Negotiations Affairs Department website http://www.nad-plo.org/inner.php?view=news-updates_pre.

[48] See http://georgewbush-whitehouse.archives.gov/news/releases/2006/05/20060523-9 html for text of joint news conference.

and air strikes. On June 10, Hamas called off its 16-month truce in response to the deaths of Palestinian civilians on a Gaza beach from Israeli artillery fire on June 9. Israel denied responsibility for the deaths, but Israeli strikes caused other Palestinian civilian casualties as well.

On June 13, Olmert told a group of British parliamentarians that, even with negotiations, "Israel will never agree to withdraw from the entire West Bank because the pre-1967 borders are not defensible." He asserted that Israel would withdraw from approximately 90% of the West Bank and that not all of Jerusalem's Arab neighborhoods would be part of the future Jewish capital.[49]

On June 28, Palestinian factions agreed on a revised National Accord Document. The Document stated that the PLO and the President of the PA will be responsible for negotiations to create a state on territories occupied by Israel in 1967. It changed the May draft to say that, in tandem with political action, resistance will be concentrated in (but not limited to) territories occupied in 1967. Signers vowed to work toward establishing a national unity government.[50] PIJ rejected the Document, while Hamas officials insisted that it did not require them to recognize Israel or to accept two states. Israel's Foreign Ministry noted that the Document did not mention recognizing Israel's right to exist or ending the conflict with Israel and argued that the return of all refugees is a formula for the destruction of Israel, contradicting a two-state solution.[51]

On June 25, members of the Hamas military wing, the Popular Resistance Committees, and the previously unknown Army of Islam had attacked Israeli forces in Israel, just outside of Gaza, killing two soldiers, wounding four, and kidnapping Corporal Gilad Shalit. On June 27, after unsuccessful diplomatic efforts to secure Shalit's release, Israel forces began a major operation to rescue him, to deter attacks, and to weaken, bring down, or change the conduct of the Hamas-led government. Israeli officials claimed that Hamas had crossed a "red line" with the kidnapping and attack within pre-1967 Israel.

On June 29, Israel forces arrested 64 Palestinian (Hamas) cabinet ministers, parliamentarians, and other Hamas officials in the West Bank and Jerusalem. On July 1, the kidnappers demanded 1,000 prisoners in exchange for the Israeli soldier. The next day, Israeli missiles destroyed the offices of the Palestinian Prime Minister. Israeli troops and tanks began sweeping northern Gaza to locate tunnels and explosives near the border and continued targeting Hamas offices in the West Bank. Hamas fired an upgraded rocket at the Israeli port city of Ashkelon prompting the Israeli cabinet to approve "prolonged" activities against Hamas.

Diplomatic efforts were undertaken to resolve the crisis. On July 10, Hamas official Mish'al insisted on the mutual release ("swap") of prisoners. Olmert rejected "trading prisoners with a terrorist bloody organization such as Hamas," adding that to negotiate with Hamas would signal that moderates such as President Abbas are not needed. The White House spokesman said that Hamas had been "complicit in perpetrating violence" and that Israel had a right to defend itself.

Although sidelined by the kidnapping, President Abbas tried to assert his power. He said that the National Accord Document would be implemented and discussed forming a national unity

---

[49] Gil Hoffman, "Olmert Bids to Enlist Chirac Support for Realignment; PM tells British MPS: Israel Would Never Agree to Withdraw to Pre-1967 Borders," *Jerusalem Post*, June 14, 2006.

[50] "Text of National Consensus Document signed by the Palestinian factions, except the Islamic Jihad Movement," *Al-Ayyam*, Open Source Center Document GMP20060628253002.

[51] For text of Foreign Ministry comments, see http://www.mfa.gov.il/mfa.

government with Hamas officials. On September 21, Abbas told the U.N. General Assembly that any future Palestinian government would commit to all prior agreements, particularly the September 1993 mutual recognition of Israel and the PLO.[52] Haniyah differed, declaring, "I personally will not head any government that recognizes Israel." Abbas concluded that efforts to form a unity government had "gone back to point zero."

On October 31, Israeli forces began a six-day incursion into Beit Hanoun in the northern Gaza Strip to stop Palestinian rocket fire; it resulted in heavy Palestinian casualties and did not stop rockets. After it ended, on November 8, an errant Israeli artillery barrage killed 20 and wounded many more, prompting international outcries. On November 25, Olmert and Abbas agreed to a cease-fire in Gaza. Hamas said that it would respect the accord, but other groups would not. The cease-fire nonetheless produced less rocket fire and shooting along the border.

On November 27, Olmert said if the Palestinians established a new government committed to carrying out the Quartet's principles, one that would implement the Road Map and bring about the release of the kidnapped soldier, then he would enter a dialogue with Abbas to establish an independent, viable Palestinian state with territorial contiguity and borders outlined by President Bush in his April 14, 2004, letter to Prime Minister Sharon. He listed other gestures Israel would make if the Palestinians recognized Israel's right to live in peace and security alongside them and renounced their demand for the right of return."[53]

Although Abbas could not meet Olmert's preconditions, the Israeli government and Bush Administration viewed him as the only partner for a peace process and took steps to bolster him in his contest with Hamas for control of the PA. On December 23, Olmert promised to hand over $100 million in tax revenue to Abbas for humanitarian purposes, to ease crossings of goods and people between Israel and the Gaza Strip, and to remove some military checkpoints in the West Bank.[54] On January 5, 2007, Olmert asserted that Israel should deal with Palestinians who are genuinely interested in peace and fight against radical forces. To that end, Israel had authorized Egypt's transfer of arms and ammunition to security forces allied with Abbas in Gaza in late December.

On January 9, the Egyptian Foreign Minister asserted that there is a common Egyptian, Jordanian, Arab, and Palestinian position that an agreement on the "end game" is needed before resuming the Road Map. Seeming to follow this line, Secretary Rice said that she would discuss "the broad issues on the horizon, so that we can work on the Road Map" with Olmert and Abbas. (The Administration reportedly had promised the "moderate" Arab regimes that it would become more engaged in the peace process in exchange for their support in countering increased Iranian influence in the region.)[55]

---

[52] "'Unofficial' Text of Palestinian President's Speech," Palestinian News Agency, September 22, 2006, BBC Monitoring Middle East.

[53] For text Olmert's speech, see Israel's MFA at http://www mfa.gov.il/MFA/Government/ Speeches+by+Israeli+leaders/2006/PM+Olmert+reaches+out+to+Palestinians+at+Ben-Gurion+memorial+27-Nov-2006 htm. For what Olmert called the "Saudi Peace Initiative, also called the "Beirut Declaration" or "Arab Peace Initiative," see http://www.saudiembassy net/2002News/Statements/StateDetail.asp?cIndex=142.

[54] On January 19, Israel transferred the funds to a special account in an Israeli bank to ensure that the money did not reach Hamas.

[55] Cam Simpson, "Dangerous Territory: With Aid, U.S. Widens Role in Palestinian Crisis; To Undercut Hamas And Iran, Bush Pushes $86 Million Plan" *Wall Street Journal*, January 12, 2007.

On February 8, Abbas designated Haniyah to form a new unity government and called on him to "*respect* international resolutions and agreements" signed by the PLO, that is, prior accords reached with Israel (italics added because it is not *accept*). Abbas's letter of designation resulted from the Mecca Accord reached at a meeting of Abbas and Hamas Political Bureau Chief Mish'al hosted by Saudi King Abdullah. The Accord aimed mainly to stop Palestinian factions' infighting and unite them in a new government; it did not refer to Israel or to the Quartet's demands.[56]

On February 19, Secretary Rice met Olmert and Abbas in Jerusalem to discuss the Mecca Accord. Afterwards, Olmert said Israel would continue to boycott the Palestinian government until it met the Quartet's demands, ended rocket attacks from Gaza, and released Shalit. Israel would not have contact with moderates in a government that does not meet the Quartet's conditions, but would maintain contact with Abbas in order to limit terror and ease Palestinian daily life. Olmert rejected negotiating with Abbas because doing so, he said, would free Hamas of the requirement to recognize Israel.

The 2002 Arab Peace Initiative was revived.[57] Following his widely reported but officially unconfirmed meeting with Saudi National Security Advisor Prince Bandar in September 2006, Olmert had noted in November 2006 that "some parts of the Saudi Peace Initiative are positive."[58] On March 11, Olmert again stated that the Saudi Initiative, on which the Arab Peace Initiative is based, is "a plan that we are ready to address seriously" and has "positive elements."

On March 15, a Palestinian unity government was formed, with a program confirming the Palestinian people's "legitimate" right of resistance, insisting that halting resistance depends on ending the occupation, the right of refugees to return to their land and belongings, and independence. The government asserted that it "respects" international resolutions and agreements signed by the PLO. At the same time, it said that it would work to consolidate the calm in Gaza, extend it to the West Bank, and transform it into a comprehensive and mutual truce. On March 17, Prime Minister Haniyah vowed to work to establish an independent Palestinian state, with Jerusalem as its capital, along the 1967 borders.[59] Hamas said that it would not recognize Israel's right to exist alongside that state. The government program authorized President Abbas to negotiate with Israel.

In response, the Israeli cabinet voted to shun all contact with the new Palestinian government until it met the Quartet's demands that it renounce violence, recognize Israel, and accept all prior accords with Israel, and called on the international community to maintain the aid embargo. The Bush Administration decided to deal with individuals in the PA government on a case-by-case basis. On March 21, Secretary Rice asserted, "We will not suspend our contacts with those in the

---

[56] Text of the Mecca Accord was published on http://www.middle-east-online.com February 9, 2007.

[57] For "Arab Peace Initiative," see http://www.al-bab.com/arab/docs/league/peace02.htm.

[58] It has been widely reported that Olmert met Saudi National Security Advisor Prince Bandar in September 2006 in Jordan. Barbara Slavin, "Arabs try Outreach to Israel, U.S. Jews...." *USA Today*, February 12, 2007, quotes former Israeli Ambassador to the United States Dani Ayalon confirming the meeting. For Olmert's speech referring to the Saudi peace initiative, see http://www mfa.gov.il/MFA/Government/Speeches+by+Israeli+leaders/2006/ PM+Olmert+reaches+out+to+Palestinians+at+Ben-Gurion+memorial+27-Nov-2006 htm.

[59] Some commentators suggest that Hamas's acceptance of a state withing the 1967 borders constitutes "implicit" recognition of Israel and that the demand for explicit recognition is "unreasonable" due to Israel's continuing occupation and failure to define its borders. Daoud Kuttab, "Obstacle or Opportunity? How the Palestinian Unity Government Offers a Path to Peace," *Washington Post*, March 26, 2007.

Palestinian government who have a record of fighting for peace."[60] A State Department spokesman said that the aid embargo would continue until the new government meets the Quartet's demands.

The Arab summit in Saudi Arabia, March 28-29, reiterated adherence, without changes, to the Arab Peace Initiative and called for direct negotiations on all tracks. Abbas voted for the Initiative, while Haniyah abstained. The Israeli Foreign Ministry stated, "Israel is sincerely interested in pursuing dialogue with those Arab states that desire peace with Israel" in order to promote a process of normalization. Prime Minister Olmert welcomed the Arabs' "revolutionary change in outlook" that represented "a new way of thinking, the willingness to recognize Israel as an established fact and to debate the conditions of the future solution" and invited all Arab heads of state, including the King of Saudi Arabia, to meet.[61] In April, an Arab League working group designated Egypt and Jordan to contact Israel. Israel expressed disappointment that League members with no formal ties to Israel would be involved, but a spokeswoman said that Israel would be "happy to hear the ideas."

In May, factional fighting in Gaza between Fatah and Hamas escalated. Later, six days of intense infighting ended with Hamas in complete control of the Gaza Strip by June 14. President Abbas declared a state of emergency, dissolved the unity government, dismissed Haniyah, and named technocrat Salam Fayyad prime minister. Hamas claimed that the decrees were illegitimate and that Haniyah was still head of government. Each side accused the other of perpetrating a coup. Secretary Rice endorsed Abbas's actions.

On June 18, President Bush told Abbas that he was open to restarting peace talks to stabilize the situation, and Israeli officials agreed that the elimination of Hamas from the Palestinian government opened "new possibilities for cooperation" and a diplomatic process. On June 25, Olmert, Abbas, Egypt's President Mubarak, and Jordan's King Abdullah II met in Sharm al Shaykh, Egypt. Abbas called on Olmert to start serious negotiations. Olmert only agreed to resume biweekly meetings with Abbas to create conditions leading to discussions on a Palestinian state. Olmert said that he would release 250 Palestinian prisoners, transfer tax revenues owed to the PA, resume security cooperation, and ease restrictions on freedom of movement in the West Bank. On July 1, Israel transferred $118 million to the PA and, on July 20, released 256 prisoners. It also granted clemency to 178 members of the Al Aqsa Martyrs' Brigades who turned in their weapons and were to be integrated into the Palestinian security force, and Israeli troops scaled back operations in the West Bank.

On June 27, the Quartet announced the appointment of former British Prime Minister Tony Blair as their Representative to help the Palestinians build the institutions and economy of a viable state in Gaza and the West Bank.

Olmert and Abbas met in Jerusalem on July 16. On July 25, Olmert confirmed that they would work on an "agreement on principles" to include the characteristics of a state, its official institutions, its economy, and customs arrangements with Israel. Olmert favored leaving "final status" issues for the end of negotiations. Abbas preferred putting the "end game" first: a Palestinian state within 1967 borders, the status of Jerusalem, and the fate of refugees, and

---

[60] "U.S. to Cut Palestinian Aid Package," Associated Press, March 22, 2007.

[61] "Israeli PM Offers Dialogue to Arabs," Associated Press, April 2, 2007.

implementation afterwards. Olmert warned Abbas that a revived Fatah-Hamas unity government would end the diplomatic process.

New Palestinian Prime Minister Fayyad presented his government's program on July 27. It stated that the government would seek to establish a state on all lands occupied by Israel in 1967, with Jerusalem as its capital and a just and agreed solution for Palestinian refugees, but did not refer to armed struggle or resistance, rather to "popular struggle against the Israeli occupation."[62]

The Bush Administration tried to show the Palestinian people that they have a choice "between the kind of chaos under Hamas in Gaza and the prospect, under President Abbas and Prime Minister Fayyad, for an effective, democratic Palestinian state," according to National Security Advisor Stephen Hadley.[63] On July 16, President Bush promised to support the reforms of Abbas and Fayyad in order to lay the foundations for serious negotiations for a Palestinian state. He called for an "international meeting this fall of representatives from nations that support a two-state solution, reject violence, recognize Israel's right to exist, and commit to all previous agreements between the parties."[64]

Olmert and Abbas worked for several months on principles to present to a U.S.-initiated international meeting in Annapolis, MD, on November 27, 2007. Abbas pressed for a framework for a substantive agreement on "core issues," formerly referred to as "final status issues," as well as for a timetable for implementation, mechanisms for implementation, and monitoring. At first, Olmert emphasized day-to-day issues, but then agreed to discuss core issues, while retaining his desire for a vague declaration without a timetable that would enable him to hold his coalition government together. On September 10, Olmert and Abbas agreed to set up negotiating teams for a two-state solution and ministerial committees to work on security, communications, economic cooperation, water rights, environmental issues, and the like, and later appointed Foreign Minister Tzipi Livni and former Prime Minister Ahmad Quray (aka Abu Ala) to head the teams.

Secretary Rice described Annapolis as a meeting at which regional actors and the international community would rally around a bilateral vision of a two-state solution as well as help support the development of Palestinian institutions, economic development, and so forth.[65] Rice excluded Hamas from the process, saying "If you're going to have a two-state solution, you have to accept the right of the other party to exist ... you're going to have to renounce violence."

On September 24, Olmert described Annapolis as a "short international meeting intended to give international encouragement to the process that we initiated with the Palestinians." He said that the goal was to increase support for Abbas and deepen Israel's ties with moderate Arab countries. Nonetheless, on October 15, Olmert suggested that it is legitimate to question whether Israel should retain outlying Palestinian neighborhoods in Jerusalem, seeming to prepare the Israeli public for concessions and raising the politically sensitive question of "dividing" Jerusalem, which many Israelis and other Jews refer to as their "eternal, undivided capital." On November

---

[62] Program of Fayyad's Government, Ma'an News Agency, July 27, 2007, BBC Monitoring Middle East, July 28, 2007.

[63] Statement on "This Week" television show, July 15, 2007, quoted in Robin Wright, "U.S. Bet on Abbas for Middle East Peace Meets Skepticism," *Washington Post*, July 16, 2007.

[64] For President's speech, see http://georgewbush-whitehouse.archives.gov/news/releases/2007/07/20070716-7.html.

[65] FM Livni's Press Conference with US Secretary of State Rice, (Israeli) Government Press Office, October 18, 2007, Open Source Center Document GMP20071018738002.

12, Olmert told his cabinet that he did not view a freeze on all building on the West Bank to be part of the Road Map's requirements, but that Israel would not build new settlements or expropriate land and would raze illegal outposts.[66] This appeared to conform to Israel's policy on so-called "natural growth," whereby settlers would be allowed to build within the borders of existing settlements. The Palestinians demand a 100% settlement freeze, including ending natural growth, and others in the international community agree with this stance.

At the Annapolis Conference on November 27, President Bush read a "Joint Understanding" that dealt with the process of negotiations, not their substance.[67] In it, Olmert and Abbas expressed determination to "immediately launch bilateral negotiations in order to conclude a peace treaty to resolve all core issues without exception, as specified in previous agreements." They agreed to engage in continuous bilateral negotiations in an effort to conclude an agreement before the end of 2008. The parties also committed to immediately implement their respective obligations under the Road Map. The parties further committed to continue implementing the Road Map until they reach a peace treaty. Implementation of the future peace treaty would be subject to the implementation of the Road Map, as judged by the United States. The United States would monitor and judge fulfillment of Road Map commitments and lead a tripartite U.S.-Israeli-Palestinian mechanism to follow up on implementation.

Both sides were able to appear successful at Annapolis. Israel succeeded in making implementation of any peace treaty dependent upon implementation of the Road Map and in avoiding a rigid timetable and deadline. It was pleased that President Bush called for Israel to be a homeland for the Jewish people, which the Palestinians have been reluctant to acknowledge because of its possible effect on the refugee issue, and for ending settlement expansion, but not for a freeze.[68] Palestinians were able to remove Road Map implementation as a precondition for final status negotiations, obtained a one-year target date, and involved United States as "judge" of the parties' fulfillment of their commitments.

General James L. Jones (Ret.) was named special envoy for Middle East security to oversee the full range of security issues for the Israelis and Palestinians and security cooperation with neighboring countries. He was tasked to design and implement a new U.S. plan for security assistance to the PA, and not to monitor compliance with the Road Map nor to replace Lt. Gen. Keith Dayton, the U.S. Middle East Security Coordinator, who had been assisting the Palestinians with improving their security forces.

On December 2, Israel published tenders for the construction of 307 new housing units in the settlement of Har Homa (Jabal abu Ghneim) in East Jerusalem. Israel maintained that, unlike the West Bank, Jerusalem is not part of the requirements of the Road Map, and that Israel would retain Har Homa in any peace accord. The PA condemned the decision and Secretary Rice criticized it.[69] Formal peace talks began on December 12. Because of the controversy over Har Homa, they were brief.

---

[66] Noam Shelef, Peace Now, informed CRS on January 30, 2008, that there are 105 illegal outposts.

[67] For text, see http://georgewbush-whitehouse.archives.gov/news/releases/2007/11/print/20071127 html. For more on the conference, seeCRS Report RS22768, *Israeli-Palestinian Peace Process: The Annapolis Conference*, by Carol Migdalovitz.

[68] For text of President Bush's remarks, see http://georgewbush.whitehouse.archives.gov/news/releases/2007/11/20071127-2 html.

[69] "James Blitz and Tobias Buck, "Israelis Criticized Over Plan to Build on Occupied Land," *Financial Times*, (continued...)

On December 30, Prime Minister Olmert directed his ministers to seek authorization from him and Defense Minister Barak for "construction, new building, expansion, preparation of plans, publication of residency tenders, and confiscation of land stemming from settlement activities in the West Bank."[70] The order did not apply to construction that had already been approved, to Jerusalem, or major settlement blocs. On February 12, 2008, the Israeli Housing Minister unveiled plans to build 1,120 new apartments in East Jerusalem. The Palestinians, who claim East Jerusalem as their future capital, condemned the action.

Before President Bush's January 2008 visit to the Middle East, National Security Advisor Stephen J. Hadley summarized three tracks to build an enduring Israeli-Palestinian peace: negotiations between Israelis and Palestinians for an outline of an agreement for a Palestinian state; implementation of the Road Map; and building institutions of a Palestinian state. Later he would say that implementation of the Road Map and standing up the institutions of a state may take longer than negotiating the outlines of a state.[71]

On January 9-10, President Bush visited Israel and the PA. On January 10, the President said that he believed that any peace agreement "will require mutually agreed adjustments to the armistice lines of 1949 to reflect current realities and to ensure that the Palestinian state is viable and contiguous." He added that new international mechanisms, including compensation, are needed to resolve the refugee issue. He observed that Jerusalem is "one of the most difficult challenges on the road to peace," but did not offer a remedy.[72] Hadley emphasized the importance of a vision of a Palestinian state and moving toward it so that, at a "moment of clarity," the Palestinian people will choose whether they want to be part of an emerging state or under the rule of Hamas.

Olmert emphasized that "as long as there will be terror from Gaza it will be very, very hard to reach any peaceful understanding between us and the Palestinians."[73] He opposed establishing two Palestinian states—a Hamas state in the Gaza Strip and a Fatah state in the West Bank.[74]

On January 3, militants fired a Katyusha rocket with a long range from Gaza into northern Ashkelon, an Israeli coastal city. On January 15, Israeli forces killed 19 Palestinians, including three civilians, in operations in Gaza. President Abbas denounced the raid as "a massacre," and, for the first time in seven months, Hamas took credit for launching rockets into Israel.

On January 17, in an effort to pressure Hamas to stop the rocket fire, Defense Minister Barak ordered the closing of border crossings from Israel into Gaza, halting supplies of fuel, leading to a major cut in electricity production from the Gaza power plant which affected water and sewage systems, hospitals, and food deliveries. Electricity deliveries from Egypt and Israel continued, and Israel said it would provide for emergency humanitarian needs. There was widespread international condemnation of Israel's action and Hamas vowed not to stop firing rockets.

(...continued)

December 8, 2007.

[70] Barak Ravid, "PM: No West Bank Construction without my Prior Approval, http://www.haaretz.com, December 31, 2007.

[71] Hadley's January 3 and 10, 2008, briefings are available at http://georgewbush-whitehouse.archives.gov/index html.

[72] Steven Lee Myers, "Bush Outlines Mideast Peace Plan," *New York Times*, January 11, 2008.

[73] Remarks by President Bush and Prime Minister Olmert in Joint Press Availability, http://georgewbush-whitehouse.archives.gov/news/releases/2008/01/20080110.html.

[74] Shahar Ilan, "Olmert Rules Out Gaza Ground Operation," *Haaretz*, January 15, 2008.

On January 23, tens of thousands of Palestinians poured out of Gaza into Egypt after Hamas militants blew holes in the border wall. Israeli officials expressed concern that more weapons would enter the Strip and called on Egypt to reestablish control over the border. According to the Egyptian foreign minister, his country wanted to reinstate arrangements for the Rafah crossing established under a 2005 agreement among Israel, Egypt, the PA, and the European Union (EU). Abbas offered to deploy his Presidential Guards to the border, but Hamas, which is physically in control of the Palestinian side of the border, insisted on participating in a new, purely Palestinian-Egyptian arrangement without an Israeli presence.[75] Abbas ruled out talks with Hamas until it gives up control of Gaza and accepts early elections. Egypt refused to cede control of the crossing to Hamas and resealed the border on February 3.

A suicide bombing killed one and injured 23 in the Israeli town of Dimona on February 4. The Hamas military wing took credit and named perpetrators from the West Bank, intending to refute Israeli allegations that the bombers had crossed from Gaza into Egypt via the open border and then infiltrated from Egypt into Israel. It was the first suicide bombing in Israel in more than a year. Israel retaliated with air strikes that killed nine Hamas militants.[76]

On February 13, Olmert suggested that, in order to avoid an impasse, it might be best to begin negotiating over borders rather than Jerusalem or refugees. On borders, he said, there are prior understandings and President Bush's April 14, 2004-letter to former Prime Minister Ariel Sharon to offer direction. Controversially, Olmert claimed an understanding with the Palestinians to delay talks on Jerusalem until the end of negotiations.[77] Palestinian official Saeb Erekat responded, "The border issue cannot advance without addressing Jerusalem's borders." Meanwhile, Foreign Minister Livni said that the talks were proceeding according the principle that "until everything is agreed on—nothing is agreed on."[78]

On January 24, the first battalion of approximately 700 Palestinian security forces crossed into Jordan to begin U.S. training for a new gendarmerie that is projected to be 5,000 strong. The effort is central to U.S./PA plans to build institutions for an eventual Palestinian state.

Violence continued. On March 6, an Arab resident of East Jerusalem killed eight students and wounded nine at a rabbinical seminary in West Jerusalem before an Israeli army officer killed him. Police attributed the attack to a lone gunman. Hamas "blessed the operation," while President Abbas condemned it.

Several Palestinian groups, including the Hamas military wing, claimed responsibility for a sniper attack near the Israel-Gaza border that wounded an aide to the Israeli Public Security Minister on April 4. On April 9, Palestinian gunmen killed two Israeli civilian employees at the Nahal Oz fuel depot, from which fuel is piped into Gaza. Israeli forces killed two of the perpetrators and an Israeli tank fired at two others, but killed three civilians and others. Israel again suspended fuel shipments to Gaza and, later, Israeli missiles struck a Hamas training site, killing two. On April 16, Hamas claimed responsibility for ambushing and killing three Israeli soldiers in the Gaza

---

[75] Joel Greenberg, "Egypt Works to Restore Breached Gaza Border," McClatchy-Tribune Service, January 27, 2008.

[76] Isabel Kershner and Taghreed El-Khodary, "Hamas Says Military Wing is Responsible for Bombing," *New York Times*, February 6, 2008.

[77] Barak Ravid and Shmuel Rosner, "Olmert: Significant Progress Possible on Borders of Palestinian State," *Haaretz*, February 13, 2008.

[78] Akiva Eldar, "Israel, PA Negotiators Oppose PM's Bid to Delay Talks on Jerusalem," *Haaretz*, February 15, 2008.

Strip as well as firing more than 20 rockets into southern Israel; Israeli retaliatory strikes, including missiles, killed 19 Palestinians.

The Hamas military wing claimed responsibility for an April 19th suicide car bombing and mortar ambush at the Kerem Shalom crossing between Israel and Gaza in which 13 Israeli soldiers were injured and the Palestinian perpetrators died. Israel retaliated with three airstrikes, killing seven Hamas militants. Five Palestinian groups claimed responsibility for killing two Israeli security guards in Tulkarem on the West Bank on April 25. Israel suspected that PIJ was responsible. On April 28, an Israeli operation against militants resulted in the deaths of a Palestinian mother and four children and the wounding of two other children. Palestinians charged that an Israeli tank shell or missile had struck the home, but an Israeli investigation suggested that explosions caused by Palestinian ammunition were the cause, not an Israeli hit.

As President Bush arrived in Israel to help celebrate its 60th anniversary on May 14, a rocket landed on a shopping mall in Ashkelon, injuring more than 30 people. PIJ and the Popular Resistance Committees claimed responsibility.

Although the two sides agreed not to make public statements about the status of their negotiations and generally kept this agreement, their officials occasionally made remarks. On February 26, Abbas reported that committees on core issues of water, borders, settlements, refugees, Jerusalem, and security had been formed. On April 18, Olmert maintained that no great gaps exist between him and Abbas "with the exception of the subject of Jerusalem, which from the outset and by agreement was deferred to a later stage."[79] On May 6, however, the PLO Executive Committee (which Abbas chairs) claimed that the gap between the two sides was "very wide" on all final status issues.[80]

On May 14, Olmert spoke of the need to reach an "understanding" that would define the parameters of a two-state solution, mentioning only the issues of borders, refugees, and security, and again suggested that it would only include "a framework for how to deal later with the issue of Jerusalem." This would have changed the approach of nothing is agreed until everything is agreed.[81]

The United States encouraged Egypt's efforts to achieve a *tahdiyah* (temporary truce, cease-fire, or calm) between Israel and Hamas. Egyptian General Omar Suleiman (alt: Umar Sulayman), who is in charge of intelligence services, mediated indirect talks. The issues involved were Palestinian rocket fire from the Gaza Strip into Israel, Israel's military operations in the Gaza Strip and West Bank and its blockade of Gaza; the border crossing at Rafah between Gaza and Egypt; Hamas's release of Cpl. Gilad Shalit; and Israel's release of Palestinian prisoners. A cease-fire to last for six months finally took effect on June 19. While Prime Minister Olmert insisted that "Shalit's release is inseparable" those the understandings, Hamas maintained that it was not and that separate talks on a prisoner exchange continued. Hamas repeatedly increased the number of prisoners whose release it demanded and those negotiations stalled. It also insisted that open border crossings were part of the cease-fire deal.

---

[79] David Landau and Yosi Verter, "An Island of Political Stability," http://www.haaretz.com, April 18, 2008.

[80] "PLO Executive Committee Denies Progress made in Negotiations with Israel," WAFA, May 6, 2008, BBC Monitoring Middle East, May 7, 2008.

[81] Herb Keinon, "PM Touts Plan that Postpones J'lem Talks," *Jerusalem Post*, May 15, 2008.

On June 24, in the first breach of the truce, the PIJ fired three rockets into Israel after Israeli troops killed a PIJ leader in Nablus on the West Bank; Israel responded by closing the commercial crossings into Gaza. That pattern continued, with smaller groups, but not Hamas, firing rockets and Israel responding with short-term closures of the crossings.

On July 25, Secretary Rice said that there was still time for Israel and the Palestinians to "reach agreement by the end of the year."[82] However, on July 28, Olmert told a Knesset committee that it was impossible to reach a comprehensive agreement in 2008 due to difficulty with and lack of negotiations on Jerusalem. He added that agreement on other issues was within reach and that a clause defining a mechanism for dealing with Jerusalem in 2009 could be included. A spokesman for Abbas again responded that an agreement excluding Jerusalem is unacceptable. On August 21, Palestinian negotiator Quray stated, "I don't think that a peace agreement can be reached by the end of this year because of the difficulties the negotiations face and also because of the internal Israeli political crisis."

On August 12, the Israeli newspaper *Haaretz* published what it said was the latest Israeli proposal for a final-status agreement. The offer called for Israel to withdraw from 93% of the West Bank and give Palestinians land equivalent to 5.5% of the West Bank in the Negev adjacent to the Gaza Strip to compensate for the less than 100% withdrawal from the West Bank. Israel would keep major settlement blocs, settlements surrounding Jerusalem, and some land in the northern West Bank bordering Israel. Israel would immediately receive the settlement blocs, but the PA would receive the land near Gaza and free passage between Gaza and the West Bank only after it retakes control of Gaza. Other settlements in the West Bank would be evacuated in two stages. After an agreement in principle, a voluntary relocation of settlers, with compensation, would be implemented. Israel would remove the remaining (est. 70,000 to 80,000) settlers when the Palestinians are capable of carrying out the entire agreement. Israel also wants the Palestinian state to be demilitarized and only accepts a Palestinian (refugee) "right of return" to the Palestinian state. The proposal does not deal with Jerusalem. *Haaretz* also reported that a Palestinian proposal called for a smaller land swap of about 2% of the West Bank and for Israel to annex only a few settlements.[83]

Palestinian negotiator Erekat dismissed the *Haaretz* report as "half-truths," stating that the Palestinians were unaware of such a proposal and would not accept a solution that excludes Jerusalem and the "right of return." Abbas's spokesman stressed that he would not accept anything less that a Palestinian state with territorial contiguity, Jerusalem as its capital, free of settlements, and on the June 4, 1967 borders.[84] Quray declared that "these leaks are untrue and were never put on the negotiating table."[85] Abbas and Palestinian negotiators oppose interim or partial agreements and insist on a comprehensive agreement on everything or no agreement at all.

In an interview published on September 29, Olmert admitted that Israel would have to give up "almost all" of the West Bank and accept the division of Jerusalem for the sake of reaching peace.

---

[82] "Rice Says Israelis, Palestinians Can Still Reach Peace Deal this Year," *Daily Star*, July 26, 2008.

[83] Aluf Benn, "Olmert to PA: We'll Quit West Bank when you Retake Gaza," http://www.haaretz.com, August 12, 2008.

[84] "Israel Must Withdraw to 1967 Borders for Peace," Al-Jazeera TV, August 12, 2008, "PA Presidential Spokesman Rejects Olmert Final Status Draft reported in *Haaretz*," WAFA, August 12, 2008, Open Source Center Document, GMP200808/12/751004.

[85] Interview with *Al-Watan*, August 20, 2008, Open Source Center Document GMP20008080820837003.

He also said that the Palestinians must receive an equal amount of Israeli territory for any West Bank land that Israel retains. Abbas disclosed that the Israeli land swap offer is 6.8% in return for 5.5% and that he rejected "offers that lead to discontinuous land areas and loss of control over water resources."[86]

On October 22, Israel and the PA reached an agreement to deploy about 550 U.S.-trained Palestinian gendarmes to Hebron.

On October 26, Foreign Minister and Olmert's replacement as Kadima Party leader Livni reported that she had been unable to form a new coalition government, thereby triggering early national elections in Israel on February 10, 2009.

On November 4, Israeli troops entered Gaza to blow up a tunnel that officials said was intended to be used to kidnap Israeli soldiers, and killed seven Palestinian militants. Officials said that the action was to eliminate a threat to the cease-fire that had begun in June and not to end it. Hamas responded by firing dozens of rockets into Israel daily and Israel reacted by closing the borders of Gaza for extended periods of time. On December 15, Hamas leaders announced that the truce would not be extended after it expired on December 19. The expiration date was followed by a barrage of rocket fire into Israel and Israeli airstrikes.

On December 27, Israel launched Operation Cast Lead with an air offensive against Hamas facilities in Gaza. The stated goal of the operation was to strike at Hamas's terrorist infrastructure and to improve security for residents of southern Israel. Israeli officials also said that they intended to regain deterrence that was widely perceived to have been weakened by the 2006 war against Hezbollah in Lebanon. The Gaza campaign broadened rapidly to target any site Israel considered part of the Hamas terrorism support network, including mosques, universities, schools, factories, homes of Hamas political and military leaders, and weapons caches. Tunnels under the Gaza-Egypt border used to smuggle arms, materiel, and goods were prime targets for the Israeli Air Force throughout the 22-day military campaign. On January 3, 2009, Israeli ground troops began to bisect the Gaza Strip.

On January 4, Israeli Prime Minister Ehud Olmert set out conditions for a cease-fire: a halt to rocket attacks and terror, international supervision of the cease-fire, and an end to Hamas's military build-up (via smuggling). Israel would not open its borders with Gaza unless Hamas released Cpl. Shalit, who was kidnapped in June 2006. On January 10, Hamas politburo chief Khalid Mish'al stated his group's counter-demands: a halt to Israel's "aggression," the immediate withdrawal of its forces from Gaza, lifting of the siege on Gaza, and opening all the crossings, foremost the Rafah crossing between Gaza and Egypt.

The Bush Administration supported Israel. From the outset, Secretary of State Rice held "Hamas responsible for breaking the cease-fire and for the renewal of violence."[87] She later said that any cease-fire should be "durable and sustainable." President Bush called the Hamas rocket attacks on Israel "an act of terror," and added that no peace deal would be acceptable without monitoring to halt the flow of smuggled weapons to the group.[88]

---

[86] Abd-al-Ra'uf Arna'ut, "President Abbas says: We are Ready to Call Simultaneous Legislative and Presidential Elections," *Al-Ayyam*, October 20, 2008, Open Source Center Document GMP20081020762002.

[87] U.S. State Department, http://2001-2009.state.gov, December 29, 2008.

[88] Margaret Coker, "Israel Ground-Invasion Threat Looms in Gaza," *Wall Street Journal*, January 3, 2009, quoting (continued...)

On January 8, the U.N. Security Council adopted Resolution 1860 by a vote of 14-0, with 1 abstention—the United States. Secretary Rice said that the United States first wanted to see the outcome of Egyptian mediation for a cease-fire. The resolution called for "an immediate, durable, and fully respected cease-fire." While emphasizing the need to alleviate the humanitarian and economic situation in Gaza, it also called for intensified efforts to sustain the cease-fire, including preventing illicit trafficking in arms and ammunition and the sustained reopening of crossing points on the basis of the 2005 Agreement on Movement and Access. Prime Minister Olmert said that the Gaza operation would continue despite the resolution because "Israel has never agreed that any outside body would determine its right to defend the security of its citizens" and because the Palestinian groups were continuing to fire rockets into southern Israel and would not honor the resolution in fact.[89] Hamas said that that the resolution had nothing to do with it because it did not meet the Palestinian people's demands and Hamas was not consulted.[90]

Egyptian mediation of a cease-fire has been stymied partly by the absence of a reconciliation between Hamas and Fatah-led PA of President Mahmud Abbas. A key issue is preventing smuggling. On January 16, Secretary Rice and Foreign Minister Livni signed a memorandum of understanding (MOU) in which they agreed to work with neighbors and others in the international community to prevent the supply of arms and related materiel to terrorist organizations. The United States vowed to work with regional and NATO partners to address the supply of arms to Hamas and others in Gaza through the Mediterranean, Gulf of Aden, Red Sea, and eastern Africa.[91] It also agreed to enhance security and intelligence cooperation to counter arms smuggling. Egyptian officials said they were was not bound by the MOU and would not allow foreign troops on their soil. Britain, France, Italy, and Germany jointly wrote to Israeli Prime Minister Olmert and Egyptian President Hosni Mubarak, offering to help end smuggling by all technical, military, naval, and diplomatic means, including patrols off Gaza's coast.

On January 17, Israel unilaterally declared a cease-fire, effective January 18. Hamas soon followed with its own one-week cease-fire. According to the U.N., which used figures provided by the Palestinian Center for Human Rights, the conflict resulted in over 1,300 Palestinian deaths and 5,400 injured, and 13 Israeli deaths (including three civilians and five soldiers from friendly fire).[92]

Israeli and Palestinian peace negotiators had said that they would continue meeting until the new U.S. Administration took office and the February 10, 2009 Israeli elections were over. However, talks were suspended several weeks before Israel launched its operation against Hamas in

---

(...continued)

President Bush's weekly radio address.

[89] "Olmert Says Israeli Army to Continue Gaza Operation Despite UN Ceasefire Resolution," *Xinhua*, January 9, 2009.

[90] "Hamas Says 'Has Nothing to do with UN Resolution 1860,'Says was not Consulted," Palestine Information Center, January 9, 2009, Open Source Center Document GMP20090109761004.

[91] Text of Memorandum of Understanding signed by US Secretary of State Rice and Israeli Foreign Minister Livni, see http://www.mfa.gov.il.

[92] Palestinian figures are from U.N. Security Council, *Update Report No. 3, Israel/Palestine: Gaza*, January 26, 2009. The IDF reported that, according to the Research Department of the Israeli Defense Intelligence, 1,166 Palestinians were killed, of whom 709 were terror operatives, as well as 295 "uninvolved Palestinians," of whom 89 were under the age of 16 and 49 women. "Majority of Palestinians Killed in Operation Cast Lead: Terror Operatives," Official website of the IDF Spokesman's Office, http://dover.idf.il/IDF/English, Open Source Center Document, GMP2009032739004, March 26, 2009.

December 2008, and formally by Palestinian chief negotiator Ahmed Quray (alternate transliteration: Qurei) on December 29.

Outgoing Prime Minister Olmert informed U.S. envoy Mitchell of "understandings" he claimed he had reached with Abbas. They included the uprooting of 60,000 settlers out of 250,000 and Israel's withdrawal to its 1967 borders, with adjustments that would allow it to retain large settlement blocs. In return for the settlement blocs, Israel would transfer an equal amount of territory in southern Israel to a Palestinian state. Olmert agreed that Jerusalem would be divided, with eastern neighborhood transferred to Palestinian sovereignty, and holy sites administered by an international authority to include Saudi Arabia, Jordan, the PA, Israel, and the United States, while Israel would retain formal sovereignty over them.[93] Israel would not absorb Palestinian refugees from 1948, but would accept a limited number in a reunification program. On January 27, Palestinian negotiator Saeb Erekat said that Olmert's proposal was never written down and its details were vague. Abbas declared, "Our stance on the peace process is clear. We want back all the territories occupied in 1967, a fair solution to the refugee issue in accordance with UN General Assembly Resolution 194, and removal of settlements. We accept an international presence in the Palestinian territories provided the Israeli army does not participate in it."[94]

After the Israeli elections, Benjamin Netanyahu was named to form a new government. On February 28, Palestinian President Mahmud Abbas said, "...we ask the Israeli government to adhere to previous agreements, not to restart from scratch, to be committed to the two-state vision, to stop settlement activity, to remove barriers, and to redeploy to the lines held prior to 28 September 2001, as stipulated in the Road Map."[95] On March 4, Palestinian negotiator Quray declared that negotiations with Israel had been suspended because of Israel's aggressive and specifically referred to its actions in East Jerusalem, where the Jerusalem municipality had given eviction orders to Palestinians in preparation for home demolitions.[96]

On March 12, Hamas issued a rare criticism of smaller groups' rocket attacks on Israel, saying that their timing was wrong—perhaps because ongoing truce talks with Israel via Egypt.[97]

On March 27, the *New York Times* reported that Israeli planes had bombed a convoy of trucks near the Egyptian border in Sudan in January that was believed to be carry arms to be smuggled into Gaza and that Iran may have sent the weapons.[98]

A new Israeli government took office on March 31. In his maiden address to the Knesset (parliament), Prime Minister Netanyahu vowed that his government would seek to attain peace with the Palestinian Authority on

---

[93] Shim'on Schiffer, "Expose: Olmert's Legacy," *Yedi'ot Aharonot*, "January 29, 2009, Open Source Center Document GMP20090129754001, Richard Boudreaux, "Olmert's Peace Bid puts Livni in a Bind," *Los Angeles Times*, February 4, 2009.

[94] "President Abbas Says: It is the Palestinian People who have Triumphed and Israel does not want Peace," *WAFA*, January 27, 2009, Open Source Center Document GMP20090127751006.

[95] "President Abbas says: We are Moving in Steady Steps towards National Reconciliation," WAFA, February 28, 2009, BBC Monitoring Middle East, March 1, 2009.

[96] "Top PLO Negotiator Suspends Talks over Jerusalem Demolitions," Ma'an News Agency, March 4, 2009, Open Source Center Document GMP20090304762002.

[97] Ibrahim Barzak, "Hamas, in Rare Move, Condemns Gaza Rocket Fire," Associated Press, March 12, 2009.

[98] Michael R. Gordon and Jeffrey Gettleman, "U.S. Officials Say Israel Struck in Sudan," *New York Times*, March 27, 2009.

three parallel channels: economic, security and diplomatic. We aspire to assist the accelerated development of the Palestinian economy, as well as of its economic ties with Israel. We will support a Palestinian security apparatus that will fight terror and we will conduct continuous peace negotiations with the Palestinian Authority with the aim of reaching a permanent arrangement.... (W)e don't want to rule over the Palestinians. Under the permanent arrangement, the Palestinians will have all the authorities to govern themselves, except those threatening the existence and security of the State of Israel.[99]

Netanyahu avoided reference to a Palestinian state. Abbas responded by saying, "This man doesn't believe in peace, so how can we deal with him," and he called on the world to exert pressure on Netanyahu.

New Israeli Foreign Minister Avigdor Lieberman raised eyebrows on April 1, when he said that the Joint Declaration presented at the Annapolis conference in 2007 is not binding because neither the Israeli government nor the Knesset ratified it. He said that Israel is bound to follow the multi-stage 2003 Performance-Based Road Map to a Permanent Two-State Solution to the Israeli-Palestinian Conflict. (See Significant Agreements, below.) The Joint Declaration called for the parties to simultaneously implement the Road Map and conduct final status negotiations. Lieberman wants to return to an incremental process, in which negotiations would be conducted in a final stage, after the Palestinians confront terror, take control of Gaza, and demilitarize Hamas.[100]

In anticipation of his May 28 meeting with President Obama, President Abbas said on May 4 that halting settlement building and the policy of house demolitions were prerequisites for a dialogue on a two-state solution.[101]

On May 4, in a speech to the American Israel Public Affairs Committee (AIPAC) Prime Minister Netanyahu restated his positions, which he described as a " fresh approach"—a triple track towards peace between Israel and the Palestinians—a political track, a security track, and an economic track. The political track means the resumption of negotiations without delay and without preconditions. The security track means continued cooperation with the U.S. program to strengthen the Palestinian security apparatus. Finally, the economic track would lead to the removal of obstacles to the advancement of the Palestinian economy. Netanyahu inserted two provisos: "peace will not come without security," and for a final peace settlement to be achieved, "the Palestinians must recognize Israel as a Jewish state,"—the nation-state of the Jewish people.[102]

Israel-Syria

Syria seeks to regain sovereignty over the Golan Heights, 450 square miles of land along the border that Israel seized in 1967. Israel applied its law and administration to the region in December 1981, an act other governments do not recognize. Approximately 20,000 Israeli settlers reside in 33 settlements on the Golan. In 1991, Syria referred to its goal in the peace conference

---

[99] Address to the Knesset by Prime Minister-designate Binyamin Netanyahu introducing Israel's 32nd Government, Channel 10 Television, March 31, 2009, Open Source Center Document GMP20090331738004.

[100] Barak Ravid, " Lieberman to *Haaretz*: Israel Ready for Mutual Peace Moves, www. haaretz.com, April 2, 2009.

[101] "Abbas Sets Tone for Talks before US Visit," *Arab News* (Jeddah), May 4, 2009.

[102] "Prime Minister Netanyahu's Speech at AIPAC," (Israeli) Government Press Office, May 5, 2009.

as an end to the state of belligerency, not a peace treaty, preferred a comprehensive Arab-Israeli peace, and rejected separate agreements between Israel and Arab states. Israel emphasized peace, defined as open borders, diplomatic, cultural, and commercial relations, security, and access to water resources.

In 1992, Israel agreed that U.N. Security Council Resolution 242 (after the 1967 war) applies to all fronts, meaning that "land for peace" includes the Golan. Syria submitted a draft declaration of principles, reportedly referring to a "peace agreement," not simply an end to belligerency. Israeli Prime Minister Yitzhak Rabin accepted an undefined withdrawal on the Golan, pending Syria's definition of "peace." On September 23, 1992, the Syrian Foreign Minister promised "total peace in exchange for total withdrawal." Israel offered "withdrawal." In 1993, Syrian President Hafez al Asad announced interest in peace and suggested that bilateral tracks might progress at different speeds. In June, U.S. Secretary of State Warren Christopher said that the United States might be willing to guarantee security arrangements in the context of a sound agreement on the Golan.

On January 16, 1994, President Clinton reported that Asad had told him that Syria was ready to talk about "normal peaceful relations" with Israel. The sides inched toward each other on a withdrawal and normalization timetable. Asad again told President Clinton on October 27 that he was committed to normal peaceful relations in return for full withdrawal. Asad never expressed his ideas publicly, leaving it to Clinton to convey them.

On May 24, 1994, Israel and Syria announced terms of reference for military talks under U.S. auspices. Syria reportedly conceded that demilitarized and thinned-out zones may take topographical features into account and be unequal, if security arrangements were equal. Israel offered Syria an early-warning ground station in northern Israel in exchange for Israeli stations on the Golan Heights, but Syria insisted instead on aerial surveillance only and that each country monitor the other from its own territory and receive U.S. satellite photographs. It was proposed that Syria demilitarize 6 miles for every 3.6 miles Israel demilitarizes. Rabin insisted that Israeli troops stay on the Golan after its return to Syria. Syria said that this would infringe on its sovereignty, but Syrian government-controlled media accepted international or friendly forces in the stations. Talks resumed at the Wye Plantation in Maryland in December 1995, but were suspended when Israeli negotiators went home after terrorist attacks in February/March 1996.

A new Israeli government led by Prime Minister Benjamin Netanyahu called for negotiations, but said that the Golan is essential to Israel's security and water needs and that retaining Israeli sovereignty over the Golan would be the basis for an arrangement with Syria. Asad would not agree to talks unless Israel honored prior understandings, claiming that Rabin had promised total withdrawal to the June 4, 1967-border, which gives Syria access to the northern shore of the Sea of Galilee (also known as Lake Tiberias or Lake Kinneret). That border differs from the international border of 1923 and the armistice line of 1949, which Damascus views as the results of colonialist or imperialist decisions.[103] Israeli negotiators say that Rabin had suggested possible full withdrawal if Syria met Israel's security and normalization needs, which Syria did not do. An Israeli law passed on January 26, 1999 requires a 61-member majority in the Knesset (parliament) and a national referendum to approve the return of any part of the Golan Heights. However, holding a referendum would depend on a passage of a Basic Law for Public Referenda, which has not been accomplished.

---

[103] Shlomo Avineri, "Only the June 4, 1967 Lines," http://www.haaretz.com, August 6, 2008.

In June 1999, Israeli Prime Minister-elect Ehud Barak and Asad exchanged compliments via a British writer. Israel and Syria later agreed to restart talks from "the point where they left off," with each side defining the point to its satisfaction. Barak and the Syrian Foreign Minister met in Washington on December 15-16, 1999, and in Shepherdstown, WV, from January 3-10, 2000. President Clinton intervened. On January 7, a reported U.S. summary revealed Israeli success in delaying discussion of borders and winning concessions on normal relations and an early-warning station. Reportedly because of Syrian anger over this leak, talks scheduled to resume on January 19, 2000 were "postponed indefinitely."

On March 26, President Clinton met Asad in Geneva. A White House spokesman reported "significant differences remain" and that it would not be productive for talks to resume. Barak indicated that disagreements centered on Israel's reluctance to withdraw to the June 1967 border and cede access to the Sea of Galilee, on security arrangements, and on the early-warning station. Syria agreed that the border/Sea issue had been the main obstacle. Asad died on June 10; his son, Bashar, succeeded him. Ariel Sharon became Prime Minister of Israel in February 2001 and vowed to retain the Golan. In a December 1 *New York Times* interview, Bashar al Asad said that he was ready to resume negotiations from where they broke off. Sharon responded that Syria first must stop supporting Hezbollah and Palestinian terror organizations.[104]

On August 29, 2005, Sharon said that it was not the time to begin negotiations with Syria because it is collaborating with Iran, building up Hezbollah, and maintaining Palestinian terrorist organizations' headquarters in Damascus from which terrorist attacks against Israel are ordered. Moreover, he observed that there was no reason for Israel to relieve the pressure that France and the United States were putting on Syria (over its alleged complicity in the February 2005 assassination of former Lebanese Prime Minister Rafik Hariri).

On June 28, 2006, Israeli warplanes caused sonic booms over President Asad's summer residence in Latakia to warn him to discontinue support for the Damascus-based head of the Hamas political bureau, Khalid Mish'al, whom Israel considered responsible for a June 25 attack in Israel, and for other Palestinian terrorists. On July 3, Syrian Foreign Minister Walid al Muallem denied that Mish'al had a role in the attack and said that Syria would never force him to leave the country.

In a speech on August 15 to mark the end of the war in Lebanon, President Asad declared that the peace process had failed since its inception and that he did not expect peace in the near future.[105] Subsequently, he said that Shib'a Farms (an area near where the Israeli, Syrian, and Lebanese borders meet) are Lebanese, but that the border between Lebanon and Syria there cannot be demarcated as long as it is occupied by Israel. The priority, he said, must be liberation.[106]

Responding to speculation about reopening peace talks with Syria, Israeli Prime Minister Olmert said on August 21 that Syria must stop supporting terrorist organizations before negotiations resume. In September, he declared, "As long as I am prime minister, the Golan Heights will remain in our hands because it is an integral part of the State of Israel."[107] He also indicated that

---

[104] See also CRS Report RL33487, *Syria: Background and U.S. Relations*, by Jeremy M. Sharp.

[105] For text of speech, see "Syria's Asad Addresses 'New Middle East,' Arab 'Failure' to Secure Peace," Syrian Arab Television TV1, Open Source Center Document GMP200608156070001.

[106] In interview by Hamdi Qandil on Dubai TV, August 23, 2006, Open Source Center Document GMP20060823650015.

[107] "Olmert Tells Israeli Paper: Golan 'An Integral Part of the State of Israel'," *Yedi'ot Aharonot*, September 26, 2006, (continued...)

he did not want to differ from the Bush Administration, which viewed Syria as a supporter of terror that should not be rewarded. On November 28, U.S. National Security Advisor Hadley concurred that as long as Syria is "a supporter of terror, is both provisioning and supporting Hezbollah and facilitating Iran in its efforts to support Hezbollah, and is supporting Hamas," then it is "not on the agenda to bring peace and security to the region." Hadley agreed that you cannot talk about negotiating with that Syria.[108]

On December 6, the Iraq Study Group released a Report that included recommendations for changing U.S. policy toward the Arab-Israeli conflict because "Iraq cannot be addressed effectively in isolation from other major regional issues." It stated that the United States will not be able to achieve its goals in the Middle East unless it has a "renewed and sustained commitment" to a comprehensive, negotiated peace on all fronts, including "direct talks with, by, and between Israel, Lebanon, Palestinians (those who accept Israel's right to exist), and particularly Syria...." The Report recommended that Israel return the Golan Heights, with a U.S. security guarantee that could include an international force on the border, including U.S. troops if requested by both parties, in exchange for Syria's taking actions regarding Lebanon and Palestinian groups.[109] Olmert rejected any linkage to the situation in Iraq and believed that President Bush shared his view.

In December, Asad and his Foreign Minister expressed interest in unconditional negotiations with Israel. Their statements deepened a debate in Israel over Syria's intentions. Olmert was skeptical of Asad's motives and demanded that Syria first end support for Hamas and Hezbollah and sever ties with Iran.[110] On January 17, 2007, Secretary Rice asserted that "this isn't the time to engage Syria," blaming Damascus for allowing terrorists to cross its territory to enter Iraq, failing to support Palestinians who believe in peace with Israel, and trying to bring down the Lebanese government.[111]

On May 4, 2007, on the sidelines of a meeting on Iraq in Egypt, Secretary Rice met Foreign Minister Muallem. U.S. officials said that the meeting focused exclusively on Iraq. Some Israelis asked why they should not have contacts with Syrians if U.S. officials could do so. On June 8, Israeli officials confirmed that Israel had sent messages to Syria signaling willingness to engage in talks based on the principle of land for peace and attempting to discern whether Damascus might be willing to gradually end its relations with Iran, Hezbollah, and Hamas in exchange.

In a July 10 interview, Olmert said that he was willing to discuss peace with Asad, but complained that the Syrian only wants negotiations to be conducted via Americans, who do not want to talk to him.[112] On July 17, Asad called on Israel to make an "unambiguous and official announcement" about its desire for peace and "offer guarantees about the return of the land in full," opening "channels via a third party, but not direct negotiations." This, he said, would lead to direct talks in the presence of an "honest broker." Those talks would be on security arrangements

---

(...continued)

citing a *Mishpaha* newspaper interview, Open Source Center Document GMP20060926746002.

[108] Shmuel Rosner, "Chirac: France, U.S. Agree There is No Point Talking to Syria," *Haaretz*, November 29, 2006.

[109] For text of Iraq Study Group report, see http://www.usip.org/isg/.

[110] Gideon Alon, "Olmert, Peretz Spar over Syrian Overtures," http://www.haaretz.com/, December 18, 2006.

[111] Interview with Andrea Mitchell of NBC News, January 17, 2007.

[112] "Israeli PM Discusses Interest in Arab Initiative, Syria Talks," Al Arabiya TV, Dubai, July 10, 2007, BBC Monitoring Middle East, July 11, 2007.

and relations, and not land. Asad asserted that he cannot negotiate with Israel because "we do not trust them."[113] On July 20, Olmert called on Asad to drop preconditions which Israel cannot accept.

On September 6, the Israeli Air Force carried out an air raid against a site in northeastern Syria. On September 12, a *New York Times* report alleged that the target may have been a nuclear weapons installation under construction with North Korean-supplied materials. Syrian and North Korean officials denied this allegation and, on October 1, President Asad claimed that an unoccupied military compound had been hit. On October 25, the International Institute for Science and International Security released satellite photos showing that a suspected reactor building had been razed and the site scraped, raising suspicions about its purpose. Syria has not retaliated for the air raid. On January 8, 2008, International Atomic Energy Agency (IAEA) Director General Mohamed El Baradei initially told a pan-Arab newspaper that, "Based on satellite photographs, experts believe it is unlikely that the targeted construction was a nuclear facility."[114] On January 12, 2008, it was reported that new satellite photos show construction at the site resembling the former building, which would cover the remains of the old one and possibly conceal its past.[115] Syria did not allow inspectors to visit the site until May. In November, the IAEA reported that it had features resembling a reactor and finding traces of uranium amid the ruins, but did not come to any conclusions. On February 24, 2009, a Syrian scientist told the IAEA that the site has been converted into a military installation for firing missiles. (See "Role of Congress/Israeli Raid on Suspected Syrian Nuclear Site," below, for additional information on this issue.)

On September 23, 2007, Secretary Rice had expressed hope that participants in the Annapolis meeting would include the members of the Arab League Follow Up Committee—12 Arab governments, including Syria. On October 1, President Asad responded that his government would not attend unless the Golan Heights were discussed.[116] Syria's Deputy Minister of Foreign Affairs attended the conference and explained that his presence resulted from the inclusion of the return of the Golan on the agenda. In December, Secretary Rice declared that "Annapolis was a chance we gave Syria and its test was the (presidential) elections in Lebanon. So far, the Syrians have failed completely."

For months, there was speculation about a revived Israel-Syria peace track as Professor Ahmet Davutoglu, a close foreign policy advisor to Turkish Prime Minister Recep Tayyip Erdogan, was reported to be carrying messages between Damascus and Jerusalem. Israeli officials repeatedly hinted that talks were afoot, acknowledging that the price of peace for Israeli would be the Golan Heights and hoping that it might be a way to distance Syria from Iran, Hezbollah, and Hamas.[117]

---

[113] Speech to People's Assembly, Syrian Arab Television, July 17, 2007, Open Source Center Document GMP20070717607001.

[114] "Report: New Satellite Photo Shows Construction at Syrian Site Bombed by Israel," Associated Press, January 12, 2008.

[115] William J. Broad, "Syria Rebuilding on Site Destroyed by Israeli Bombs," *New York Times*, January 12, 2008.

[116] "Assad Casts Doubt on Syrian Participation in Peace Summit," Associated Press, October 11, 2007, citing an interview with Tunisian newspapers.

[117] Herb Keinon and Yaakov Katz, "Olmert Hints at Secret Syria Track," *Jerusalem Post*, March 27, 2008, Mark Weiss, "Barak: Renewing Peace Talks with Damascus is a Priority; Assad (sic) Accuses Israel of Foot-Dragging in Negotiations," *Jerusalem Post*, March 30, 2008.

On April 17, Prime Minister Olmert confirmed that the two sides had been in contact and, on April 24, President Asad revealed that Erdogan had informed him "about Israel's readiness for a full withdrawal from the Golan Heights in return for a peace agreement." Asad claimed that mediation had intensified after the Israel-Hezbollah war of 2006 and especially after Turkey became involved in April 2007. Reports said that Olmert had first discussed the possibility of mediation with Erdogan in Turkey in February 2007. Asad also asserted that there would be no direct negotiations, only those through Turkey. He maintained that direct talks require a U.S. sponsor and that Syria might discuss them "with the next U.S. administration because this one has no vision or a will for the peace process."[118] U.S. State Department spokesman Tom Casey has said that neither party has formally requested the United States to become directly involved. "If Syria and Israel came to us, we'd certainly consider the request."[119]

On May 21, Israel, Syria, and Turkey simultaneously announced that Israel and Syria had indeed launched peace talks mediated by Turkey. On May 19-21, negotiating teams had held indirect talks in Istanbul. The aim was to reach "common ground" on issues relating to withdrawal, security arrangements, water, and normal peaceful relations from which to move toward direct negotiations.

This initiative appeared contrary to the Bush Administration's policy of isolating Syria. However, the White House said that the Administration was not surprised by the trilateral announcement and did not object to it. Secretary Rice said, "We would welcome any steps that might lead to a comprehensive peace in the Middle East .... We are working very hard on the Palestinian track. It doesn't mean that the U.S. would not support other tracks." White House spokeswoman Dana Perino added, "What we hope is that this is a forum to address various concerns that we all share about Syria – the United States, Israel, and many others – in regard to Syria's support for Hamas and Hezbollah (and) the training and funding of terrorists that belong to these organizations .... We believe it could help us to further isolate Iran...."[120] On June 5, Secretary Rice thanked Turkey for sponsoring the indirect talks.

Asad stated that direct talks are unlikely before 2009 and "depend on the stability of the Israeli government...."[121] He said that eventually direct negotiations would tackle the details of water, relations, and other matters, but, when dealing with water, Syria would never compromise on the 1967 borders that stretch to Lake Tiberias (the Sea of Galilee). Referring to Israel's demands concerning Syria's relations with Iran and Hezbollah, Asad asserted, "We do not accept the imposition of conditions on us that are linked to countries that have nothing to do with peace...."[122] On July 7, Asad told the French newspaper *Le Figaro* that he would not begin direct talks with Israel while President Bush is in office.[123]

---

[118] "Al-Asad Reveals Turkish Mediation with Israel," *Al-Watan*, April 24, 2008, Open Source Center Document GMP20080424090001, also interview with Asad by editors of *Al-Watan*, April 27, 2008, Open Source Center Document FEA20080429651667.

[119] Jay Solomon, "Syria calls for U.S. to Play a Direct Role in Peace Talks," *Wall Street Journal*, June 2, 2008.

[120] Cam Simpson, " Israel, Syria in Indirect Peace Talks," *Wall Street Journal*, May 22, 2008, "US Welcomes Syrian-Israeli Talks but Stresses Palestinian Track," Yahoo! News, May 21, 2008, "Rice: Israeli-Palestinian Track Most Likely to Produce Results," Associated Press, May 22, 2008.

[121] "Syria says No Direct Talks with Israel before 2009," *Times of Oman*, June 4, 2008, citing *Al-Khaleej* Emirates daily.

[122] "Syria says Israel Terms Signal not Serious on Peace," Reuters, June 5, 2008.

[123] Barak Ravid, "Assad: Direct Talks with Israel Only After Bush Leaves Office," *Haaretz*, July 8, 2008.

On September 4, President Asad disclosed that his representatives had transmitted proposals or principles for peace to serve as a basis for direct talks with Israel to Turkish mediators, but would wait for Israel's response before holding direct talks. He repeated that direct talks also await a new U.S. Administration and stressed that "Syria has no interest in relinquishing its ties with Hezbollah."[124] He added that future negotiations depend on the next Israeli prime minister's commitment to pursuing peace. A fifth round of indirect talks was postponed ostensibly due to the resignation of Yoram Turbowicz, Olmert's chief of staff and negotiator with Syria. The Turkish government said that Israel had requested a delay due to technical and legal problems.

Syria's Deputy Foreign Minister reported that Syria had asked Israeli to express a final opinion about the line of withdrawal and insisted that it be on the June 4, 1967 border. Israeli military intelligence reportedly has concluded that, under the next U.S. administration, Syria would be willing to sign a peace accord with Israel if a return to the 1967 border is guaranteed and if it includes generous U.S. economic aid comparable to that which Egypt has received since signing a peace agreement with Israel. The analysts also believe that Syria would be willing to "cool down" its relations with Iran as the price of an accord.[125]

As a result of Israel's offensive against Hamas, Turkey officially ended its efforts to organize additional peace talks between Israel and Syria. The talks already had been suspended primarily due to Israel's domestic political turmoil and imminent national election on February 10, 2009. On February 2, however, Foreign Minster Muallem said that Syria may resume indirect talks with Israel if its elections bring forth a government willing to reach a comprehensive peace.[126]

While in Turkey on March 7, Secretary of State Clinton said the importance of the Israeli-Syrian track and peace effort "cannot be overstated."[127] In Damascus the same day, Acting Assistant Secretary of State for Near Eastern Affairs Jeffrey Feltman said, "We do want to see forward momentum on the Syrian-Israeli track at the time when the parties are ready for this. We want to achieve results. I am sure that Syria will want to achieve results, but let's not expect that things are going to change dramatically from today until tomorrow."[128]

In an interview published on March 9, Syrian President Bashar al Asad said that a peace "agreement" with Israel was possible, but that the Syrian people would not accept "peace," meaning trade, normal relations, and open borders, until the Palestinian issue is resolved. He called for coordination with the Palestinians so that Israel would not use peace talks with Syria to avoid a resolution with the Palestinians.[129] Two days later, Asad reiterated his long-standing view that, "We need the United States to act as a mediator when we move from the current indirect negotiations to direct negotiations."[130] In a speech to the Arab League summit in Doha, Qatar on March 31, he called on Arabs to change their tactics and take a harder line to cope with the

---

[124] "Herb Keinon, "Frustrated Israel watches Syria Break Out of Isolation," *Jerusalem Post*, September 5, 2008.

[125] Amir Rapaport, "IB Estimate: Syria's Peace Intentions are Serious," *Ma'ariv*, October 23, 2008, BBC Monitoring Middle East, October 24, 2008.

[126] Mary Fitzgerald, "Syria to Decide on Talks with Tel Aviv after Israeli Poll," *Irish Times*, February 3, 2009.

[127] Natasha Mozgovaya, "Clinton Encourages Israel-Syria Peace Talks," http://www.haaretz.com, March 7, 2009.

[128] Khaled Yacoub Oweis, "U.S. Officials Find 'Common Ground' in Syria," Reuters, March 7, 2009.

[129] "Peace with Israel Possible, Says Syria's Assad," Reuters, March 9, 2009.

[130] Interview quoted by Yoav Stern, "Assad: Direct Israel Talks Possible if U.S. Mediates," www. haaretz.com, March 11, 2009.

incoming Israeli government, and stated, "Peace cannot be achieved with an enemy who does not believe in peace without it begin imposed on him by resistance"—a "moral duty."

Israeli Foreign Minister Avigdor Lieberman said on April 2, "there is no (Israeli) cabinet resolution regarding negotiations with Syria, and we have already said that we will not agree to withdraw from the Golan Heights. Peace will only be in exchange for peace."[131] On May 20, Prime Minister Netanyahu said that he was willing to open peace talks with the Syrians without preconditions.[132] Syria has said that Israel must commit to ceding the Golan before talks.

Israel-Lebanon

Citing Security Council Resolution 425, Lebanon sought Israel's unconditional withdrawal from the 9-mile "security zone" in southern Lebanon, and the end of Israel's support for Lebanese militias in the south and its shelling of villages that Israel claimed were sites of Hezbollah activity. Israel claimed no Lebanese territory, but said that its forces would withdraw only when the Lebanese army controlled the south and prevented Hezbollah attacks on northern Israel. Lebanon sought a withdrawal schedule in exchange for addressing Israel's security concerns. The two sides never agreed. Syria, which then dominated Lebanon, said that Israel-Syria progress should come first. Israel's July 1993 assault on Hezbollah prompted 250,000 people to flee from south Lebanon. U.S. Secretary of State Warren Christopher arranged a cease-fire. In March/April 1996, Israel again attacked Hezbollah and Hezbollah fired into northern Israel. Hezbollah and the Israeli Defense Forces agreed to a cease-fire and to refrain from firing from or into populated areas but retained the right of self-defense. U.S., French, Syrian, Lebanese, and Israeli representatives monitored the agreement.

On January 5, 1998, the Israeli Defense Minister indicated readiness to withdraw from southern Lebanon if the second part of Resolution 425, calling for the restoration of peace and security in the region, were implemented. He and Prime Minister Netanyahu proposed withdrawal in exchange for security, not peace and normalization. Lebanon and Syria called for an unconditional withdrawal. As violence in northern Israel and southern Lebanon increased later in 1998, the Israeli cabinet twice opposed unilateral withdrawal. In April 1999, however, Israel decreased its forces in Lebanon and, in June, the Israeli-allied South Lebanese Army (SLA) withdrew from Jazzin, north of the security zone. On taking office, new Israeli Prime Minister Ehud Barak promised to withdraw in one year, by July 7, 2000.

On September 4, 1999, the Lebanese Prime Minister confirmed support for the "resistance" against the occupation, that is, Hezbollah. He argued that Palestinian refugees residing in Lebanon have the right to return to their homeland and rejected their implantation in Lebanon (which would upset its fragile sectarian balance). He also rejected Secretary of State Madeleine Albright's assertion that refugees would be a subject of Israeli-Palestinian final status talks and insisted that Lebanon be a party to such talks.

On March 5, 2000, the Israeli cabinet voted to withdraw from southern Lebanon by July. Lebanon warned that it would not guarantee security for northern Israel unless Israel also withdrew from the Golan and worked to resolve the refugee issue. On April 17, Israel informed the U.N. of its plan. On May 12, Lebanon told the U.N. that Israel's withdrawal would not be complete unless it

---

[131] Ravid, April 2, 2009, op. cit.

[132] Isabel Kershner, "Netanyahu Says He's Willing to Talk with Syria," *New York Times*, May 21, 2009.

included Shib'a Farms. On May 23, U.N. Secretary-General Kofi Annan noted that most of Shib'a is within the area of operations of the U.N. Disengagement Observer Force (UNDOF) overseeing the 1974 Israeli-Syrian disengagement, and recommended proceeding without prejudice to later border agreements. On May 23, the SLA collapsed, and on May 24 Israel completed its withdrawal. Hezbollah took over the former security zone. On June 18, the U.N. Security Council agreed that Israel had withdrawn. The U.N. Interim Force in Lebanon (UNIFIL) deployed only 400 troops to the border region because the Lebanese army did not back them against Hezbollah.[133]

On October 7, Hezbollah shelled northern Israel and captured three Israeli soldiers; then, on October 16, it captured an Israeli colonel. On November 13, the U.N. Security Council said that Lebanon was obliged to take control of the area vacated by Israel. On April 16 and July 2, 2001, after Hezbollah attacked its soldiers in Shib'a, Israel, claiming that Syria controls Hezbollah, bombed Syrian radar sites in Lebanon. In April, the U.N. warned Lebanon that unless it deployed to the border, UNIFIL would be cut or phased out. On January 28, 2002, the Security Council voted to cut it to 2,000 by the end of 2002.

In March 2003, Hezbollah shelled Israeli positions in Shib'a and northern Israel. Israel responded with air strikes and expressed concern about a possible second front in addition to the Palestinian *intifadah*. At its request, the U.N. Secretary-General contacted the Syrian and Lebanese Presidents and, on April 8, Vice President Cheney telephoned President Asad and Secretary of State Powell visited northern Israel and called on Syria to curb Hezbollah. On January 30, 2004, Israel and Hezbollah exchanged 400 Palestinian and 29 Lebanese and other Arab prisoners, and the remains of 59 Lebanese for the Israeli colonel and the bodies of the three soldiers.

U.N. Security Council Resolution 1559, September 2, 2004, called for the withdrawal of all foreign (meaning Syrian) forces from Lebanon.[134] Massive anti-Syrian demonstrations occurred in Lebanon after the February 14, 2005, assassination of former Lebanese Prime Minister Rafik Hariri, widely blamed on Syrian agents. On March 5, Asad announced a phased withdrawal of Syrian troops from Lebanon, which was completed on April 26.

On May 28, 2006, Palestinian rockets fired from Syria hit deep inside northern Israel and Israeli planes and artillery responded by striking Popular Front for the Liberation of Palestine-General Command (PFLP-GC) bases near Beirut and near the Syrian border. Hezbollah joined the confrontation and was targeted by Israelis. UNIFIL brokered a cease-fire.

On July 12, in the midst of massive shelling of a town in northern Israel, Hezbollah forces crossed into northwestern Israel and attacked two Israeli military vehicles, killing three soldiers and kidnapping two. Hezbollah demanded that Israel release Lebanese and other Arab prisoners in exchange for the soldiers and for a third soldier who had been kidnapped by the Palestinian group Hamas on June 25. (On the latter situation, see "Israel-Palestinians," above.) Hezbollah leader Shaykh Hassan Nasrallah said that the soldiers would be returned only through indirect negotiations for a prisoner exchange. He suggested that the Hezbollah operation might provide a way out of the crisis in Gaza because Israel had negotiated with Hezbollah in the past, although it refused to negotiate with Hamas now.

---

[133] See CRS Report RL31078, *The Shib'a Farms Dispute and Its Implications*, by Alfred B. Prados.

[134] For text of U.N. Security Council Resolution 1559, see http://www.un.org/Docs/sc/unsc_resolutions04.html.

Prime Minister Olmert declared that Hezbollah's attack was "an act of war" and promised that Lebanon would suffer the consequences of Hezbollah's actions. The Lebanese government replied that it had no prior knowledge of the operation and did not take responsibility or credit for it. Israeli officials also blamed Syria and Iran, but were careful to say that they had no plans to strike either one. Immediately after the Hezbollah attack, Israeli forces launched a major military campaign against and imposed an air, sea, and ground blockade on Lebanon. In a July 17 speech, Olmert summarized Israel's conditions for the end of military operations: the return of the kidnapped soldiers, the end to Hezbollah rocket attacks, and the deployment of the Lebanese army along the border.[135]

Lebanese Prime Minister Fuad Siniora requested U.N. help in arranging a cease-fire. On August 8, the Lebanese government promised to deploy 15,000 troops to the south for the first time since 1978 if Israel withdrew its forces. Hezbollah agreed to the government proposal, while Olmert found it "interesting." On August 9, the Israeli security cabinet authorized the Prime Minister and Defense Minister to determine when to expand the ground campaign while continuing efforts to achieve a political agreement. Only after the U.N. Security Council passed Resolution 1701 calling for the end to hostilities on August 11 did Olmert authorize an offensive, and those two days of fighting proved costly for both sides ensued.

Resolution 1701 called for the full cessation of hostilities, the extension of the Lebanese government's control over all Lebanese territory, and the deployment of Lebanese forces and an expanded UNIFIL, 15,000 each, in a buffer zone between the Israeli-Lebanese border and the Litani River to be free of "any armed personnel" other than the Lebanese army and UNIFIL.[136] The resolution authorized UNIFIL to ensure that its area of operations is not used for hostile activities and to resist by forceful means attempts to prevent it from discharging its duties. It banned the supply of arms to Lebanon, except as authorized by the government, and called for the disarmament of all armed groups in Lebanon. The resolution did not require the return of the abducted Israeli soldiers or the release of Lebanese prisoners. It requested the Secretary-General to develop proposals for the delineation of the international borders of Lebanon, "including by dealing with the Shib'a Farms area." The truce went into effect on August 14. In all, 44 Israel civilians and 119 military men, 1,191 Lebanese civilians, 46 Lebanese soldiers, and an estimated 600 Hezbollah militants died in the war. The Lebanese Army began to move south to the border on August 17 as Israeli forces handed over positions to the U.N.

Hezbollah leader Nasrallah declared victory and said that Hezbollah would not disarm as long as Israel did not withdraw completely from Lebanon, including the Shib'a Farms. On August 14, the Lebanese Defense Minister said that his army had no intention of disarming Hezbollah, but Hezbollah weapons would no longer be visible. On August 19, Israeli commandos raided an Hezbollah stronghold near Ba'albek in the Bekaa Valley. Hezbollah did not respond and the cease-fire held.

Olmert accepted responsibility for the war and claimed as achievements a terrorist organization no longer allowed to operate from Lebanon and a government of Lebanon responsible for its territory. He also claimed that a severe blow had been dealt to Hezbollah.[137] After the war, Olmert

---

[135] For text of Olmert's speech, as carried on Israel Television Channel 1, see Open Source Center Document GMP20060717740013, July 17, 2006.

[136] Text of U.N. Security Council Resolution 1701 is accessible online at http://www.un.org/Docs/sc/ unsc_resolutions06 htm.

[137] For text of Olmert's statement, see Israeli Television Channel 1, August 14, 2006, Open Source Center Document (continued...)

expressed hope that the cease-fire could help "build a new reality between Israel and Lebanon," while Prime Minister Siniora declared that Lebanon would be the last country to sign a peace agreement with Israel. On September 7, Olmert said that if the Shib'a Farms is determined to be Lebanese and not Syrian and if Lebanon fulfills its obligations under U.N. resolutions, including the disarming of Hezbollah, then Israel would discuss the Farms with Lebanon.

On October 30, the U.N. Secretary-General Ban Ki-moon reported that there has been no breach of the 2006 cease-fire and that the parties show determination to keep it. He noted reports of suspected Hezbollah construction north of the Litani River and in the Bekaa Valley, and stated that the Israeli government contends that Hezbollah has rearmed itself to a level higher than prior to the 2006 conflict because of the transfer of weapons from Iran and Syria in violation of the arms embargo.[138]

On February 12, 2008, Hezbollah operative Imad Mughniyah, who was suspected of planning terrorist attacks in the 1980s against Americans in Lebanon and in the 1990s against Jews and Israelis in Argentina, was killed in a car bombing in Damascus, Syria.

On May 31, Hezbollah handed over to Israel the remains of five soldiers killed in the summer war of 2006, and Israel released an Israeli of Lebanese descent who had been convicted of spying for Hezbollah. On June 29, the Israeli cabinet approved a larger prisoner exchange with Hezbollah. The remains of two Israeli soldiers whose capture by Hezbollah had triggered the 2006 war, a report on Ron Arad, an Israeli pilot missing in action since 1986, and the remains of Israeli soldiers killed in the 2006 war were given to Israel. In exchange, Israel released Samir Kuntar, a Lebanese member of a Palestinian terrorist group who had killed an Israeli man and his young daughter in 1979, four Hezbollah fighters, the bodies of eight Hezbollah members, and the bodies of other terrorists, and information on four missing Iranian diplomats to the U.N. Secretary General. At a later date, Israel released some Palestinian prisoners.

During a visit to Lebanon, Secretary Rice called for U.N. action on Shib'a Farms. Hezbollah has used that Israeli occupation to justify its "resistance" and rejection of disarmament, but says that putting the Farms in U.N. custody will not end its resistance. On June 18, Israel offered to start direct peace talks on all issues with Lebanon. The Lebanese government rejected the offer, stating that occupied Lebanese territory is subject to "U.N. resolutions that do not require any negotiations."[139] Beirut demanded that Israel return Shib'a and provide maps of mines and cluster bombs left during the 2006 war.

On July 13, new Lebanese President Michel Suleiman said the Shib'a Farms area should be liberated through diplomatic means, but, if diplomacy fails, military operations would be used. On August 13, he and Syrian President Asad stated that a committee would work to "define and draw the Syrian-Lebanese borders," but Shi'ba Farms will not be demarcated until Israel withdraws.[140]

(...continued)

GMP20060814728001.

[138] United Nations Security Council, *Report of the Secretary General on the Implementation of Security Council Resolution 1701 (2006)*, S/2007/641, October 30, 2007, accessible via http://www.un.org/Docs/sc/sgrep07.htm.

[139] "Beirut Reiterates Rejection of Bilateral Talks over Shebaa," *Daily Star*, June 19, 2008.

[140] Khaled Yacoub Oweis, "Syria and Lebanon to Work on Drawing Border," Reuters, August 14, 2008.

On September 4, Hezbollah leader Nasrallah declared that his group would not disarm even if Israel withdrew from the Shib'a Farms and the northern Ghajar village because its weapons are needed to defend Lebanon from Israel.[141] In his November 18, Report to the Security Council, Secretary-General Ban Ki-moon noted that there had been no breaches of the cessation of hostilities. He again cited Israeli concerns that Hezbollah was rebuilding its military capacity on both sides of the Litani River, but noted that UNIFIL had not been provided with nor found evidence of new military infrastructures or smuggling arms in its area of operation.[142] The Secretary-General also noted that Hezbollah continued to maintain a substantial military capacity distinct from the Lebanese state in contravention of 1701. In addition, he called on Israel to cease all over flights of Lebanese territory that violate Lebanese sovereignty and 1701.

On March 18, 2009, President Suleiman ruled out the possibility that his country would hold direct peace talks with Israel, saying that a regional conference would be the best way to resolve differences between the two neighbors.

Israel-Jordan

Of Jordan's 3.4 million people, 55 to 70% are Palestinian. Jordan initialed a June 1993 agenda with Israel on water, energy, environment, and economic matters on September 14, 1993. On July 25, 1994, Israeli Prime Minister Yitzhak Rabin and King Hussein signed the Washington Declaration, a non-belligerency accord. A peace treaty was signed on October 26, 1994. (See "Significant Agreements," below). The border was demarcated and Israel withdrew from Jordanian land on February 9, 1995. More agreements followed.

Although supportive of the peace process and of normalization of relations with Israel, on March 9, 1997, King Hussein charged that Israeli Prime Minister Benjamin Netanyahu was "bent on destroying the peace process...." After Israeli agents bungled an attempt to assassinate Hamas official Khalid Mish'al in Jordan on September 25, 1997, the King demanded that Israel release Hamas founder Shaykh Yassin, which it did on October 1, with 70 Jordanian and Palestinian prisoners in exchange for the detained Israeli agents. On December 5, 1998, the King called for Jordanian-Palestinian coordination, observing that many final status issues are Jordanian national interests. King Hussein died on February 7, 1999, and was succeeded by his son Abdullah.

King Abdullah II said that the Palestinians should administer the Muslim holy sites in Jerusalem, a traditional responsibility of his family, and proposed that Jerusalem be an Israeli and a Palestinian capital, but rejected a Jordanian-Palestinian confederation. Until Israel and the Palestinians reach an accord, however, Jordan insists on its right to maintain and oversee the holy sites. On November 21, 2000, Jordan stopped accreditation of a new ambassador to Israel because of Israeli "aggression" against the Palestinians. On March 18, 2004, the King met Prime Minister Sharon to discuss Israel's security barrier and disengagement from Gaza. In February 2005, Jordan sent an ambassador to Israel; in March, its foreign minister visited Israel for the first time in four years.

---

[141] For background see CRS Report R40054, *Lebanon: Background and U.S. Relations*, by Casey L. Addis.

[142] Report of the Secretary-General on Implementation of Security Council Resolution 1701 (2006), S/2008/715, November 18, 2008, accessible via http://www.un.gov.

In a March 14, 2007, address to a joint session of Congress, the King pleaded for U.S. leadership in the peace process, which he called the "core issue in the Middle East." He suggested that the Arab Peace Initiative is a path to achieve a collective peace treaty.

Significant Agreements and Documents

Israel-PLO Mutual Recognition

On September 9, 1993, PLO Chairman Yasir Arafat recognized Israel's right to exist, accepted U.N. Security Council Resolutions 242 and 338, the Middle East peace process, and the peaceful resolution of conflicts. He renounced terrorism and violence and undertook to prevent them, stated that articles of the Palestinian Charter that contradict his commitments are invalid, undertook to submit Charter changes to the Palestine National Council, and called upon his people to reject violence. Israeli Prime Minister Yitzhak Rabin recognized the PLO as the representative of the Palestinian people and agreed to negotiate with it.[143]

Declaration of Principles

On August 29, 1993, Israel and the Palestinians announced that they had agreed on a Declaration of Principles on interim self-government for the West Bank and Gaza, after secret negotiations in Oslo, Norway, since January 1993. Effective October 13, it called for Palestinian self-rule in Gaza and Jericho; transfer of authority over domestic affairs in the West Bank and Gaza to Palestinians; election of a Palestinian Council with jurisdiction over the West Bank and Gaza. During the interim period, Israel is to be responsible for external security, settlements, Israelis in the territories, and foreign relations. Permanent status negotiations to begin in the third year of interim rule and may include Jerusalem.[144]

Agreement on the Gaza Strip and the Jericho Area

Signed on May 4, 1994, provides for Israeli withdrawal from Gaza/Jericho, and describes the Palestinian Authority's (PA) responsibilities. The accord began the five-year period of interim self-rule.[145]

Israel-Jordan Peace Treaty

Signed on October 26, 1994.

Israeli-Palestinian Interim Agreement, West Bank-Gaza Strip

(Also called the Taba Accords or Oslo II.) Signed on September 28, 1995. Annexes deal with security arrangements, elections, civil affairs, legal matters, economic relations, Israeli-

---

[143] For text, see http://2001-2009.state.gov/p/nea/rls/22579 htm.

[144] For text, see http://2001-2009.state.gov/p/nea/rls/22602 htm.

[145] For text, see http://2001-2009.state.gov/p/nea/rls/22676 htm.

Palestinian cooperation, and the release of prisoners. Negotiations on permanent status to begin in May 1996. An 82-member Palestinian Council and Head of the Council's Executive Authority will be elected after the Israeli Defense Force redeploys from Jenin, Nablus, Tulkarem, Qalqilyah, Ramallah, and Bethlehem, and 450 towns and villages. Israel will redeploy in Hebron, except where necessary for security of Israelis. Israel will be responsible for external security and the security of Israelis and settlements. Palestinians will be totally responsible for Area "A," the six cities, plus Jericho. Israeli responsibility for overall security will have precedence over Palestinian responsibility for public order in Area "B," Palestinian towns and villages. Israel will retain full responsibility in Area "C," unpopulated areas. Palestinian Charter articles calling for the destruction of Israel will be revoked within two months of the Council's inauguration.[146]

Protocol Concerning the Redeployment in Hebron

Initialed by Israel and the PA on January 15, 1997. Details security arrangements. Accompanying Israeli and Palestinian Notes for the Record and letter from Secretary of State Christopher to Prime Minister Netanyahu.[147]

Wye River Memorandum

Signed on October 23, 1998. Delineated steps to complete implementation of the Interim Agreement and of agreements accompanying the Hebron Protocol. Israel will redeploy from the West Bank in exchange for Palestinian security measures. The PA will have complete or shared responsibility for 40% of the West Bank, of which it will have complete control of 18.2%. The PLO Executive and Central Committees will reaffirm a January 22, 1998, letter from Arafat to President Clinton that specified articles of the Palestinian Charter that had been nullified in April 1996. The Palestine National Council will reaffirm these decisions. President Clinton will address this conclave.[148]

Sharm al Shaykh Memorandum

(Also called Wye II.) Signed on September 4, 1999.[149] Israeli Prime Minister Barak and PA Chairman Arafat agreed to resume permanent status negotiations in an accelerated manner in order to conclude a framework agreement on permanent status issues in five months and a comprehensive agreement on permanent status in one year. Other accords dealt with unresolved matters of Hebron, prisoners, etc.

A Performance-Based Road Map to a Permanent Two-State Solution to the Israeli-Palestinian Conflict

(More briefly referred to as the Road Map.) Presented to Israel and the Palestinian Authority on April 30, 2003, by the Quartet (i.e., the United States, European Union, United Nations, and Russia). To achieve a comprehensive settlement in three phases by 2005. Phase I calls for the

---

[146] For text, see http://2001-2009.state.gov/p/nea/rls/22678 htm.

[147] For Protocol text, see http://2001-2009.state.gov/p/nea/rls/22680 htm.

[148] For text, see http://2001-2009.state.gov/p/nea/rls/22694 htm.

[149] For text, see http://2001-2009.gov/p/nea/rls/22696.htm.

Palestinians to unconditionally end violence, resume security cooperation, and undertake political reforms, and for Israel to withdraw from areas occupied since September 28, 2000, and to freeze all settlement activity. Phase II will produce a Palestinian state with provisional borders. Phase III will end in a permanent status agreement which will end the conflict.[150]

Agreement on Movement and Access

From the Gaza Strip, reached on November 15, 2005, calls for reopening the Rafah border crossing to Egypt with European Union monitors on November 25, live closed circuit TV feeds of the crossing to Israel, Palestinian bus convoys between the West Bank and Gaza beginning December 15, exports from Gaza into Israel, and construction of the Gaza seaport.[151]

Joint Understanding

Read by President Bush at the Annapolis Conference, November 27, 2007. Prime Minister Olmert and President Abbas express their determination to immediately launch continuous, bilateral negotiations in an effort to conclude a peace treaty resolving all core issues before the end of 2008. They also commit to immediately and continuously implement their respective obligations under the Road Map until they reach a peace treaty. Implementation of the peace treaty will be subject to the implementation of the Road Map, as judged by the United States.[152]

Role of Congress

Aid

Foreign aid issues related to the peace process are covered extensively in other CRS reports. For details, please see CRS Report RS22967, *U.S. Foreign Aid to the Palestinians*, by Jim Zanotti, and CRS Report RL33222, *U.S. Foreign Aid to Israel*, by Jeremy M. Sharp, CRS Report RL32260, *U.S. Foreign Assistance to the Middle East: Historical Background, Recent Trends, and the FY2009 Request*, by Jeremy M. Sharp.

In general, in order to ensure that Israel has a partner for peace, Congress has provide assistance for the development of Palestinian institutions, security forces, and democracy, including language that prohibits any assistance for Hamas unless it meets international conditions with respect to Israel, and requires good governance practices. It also has appropriated considerable military assistance for Israel and included language ensuring Israel's "qualitative military edge" over its regional neighbors. Congress also has increased aid to Jordan, in part to short up its position as a voice of moderation and for peace in the region.

---

[150] For text, see http://2002-2009.state.gov/r/pa/prs/ps/2003/20062.htm.

[151] For text, see http://www.israel-mfa.gov.il/MFA/Peace+Process/Reference+Documents/Agreed+documents+on+movement+and+access+from+and+to+Gaza+15-Nov-2005 htm.

[152] For text, see http://georgewbush-whitehouse.archives.gov/news/releases/2007/11/20071127.html.

Jerusalem

Israel annexed the city in 1967 and proclaimed it to be Israel's eternal, undivided capital. Palestinians seek East Jerusalem as their capital. Successive U.S. Administrations have maintained that the parties must determine the fate of Jerusalem in negotiations. H.Con.Res. 60, June 10, 1997, and S.Con.Res. 21, May 20, 1997, called on the Administration to affirm that Jerusalem must remain the undivided capital of Israel. Congress has repeatedly prohibited official U.S. government business with the Palestinian Authority (PA) in Jerusalem and the use of appropriated funds to create U.S. government offices in Israel to conduct business with the PA and allows Israel to be recorded as the place of birth of U.S. citizens born in Jerusalem. These provisions are again in P.L. 111-8, the Omnibus Appropriations Act, 2009, signed into law on March 11, 2009. The State Department does not recognize Jerusalem, Israel as a place of birth for passports because the U.S. government does not recognize all of Jerusalem as part of Israel.

A related issue is the relocation of the U.S. embassy from Tel Aviv to Jerusalem. Proponents argue that Israel is the only country where a U.S. embassy is not in the capital, that Israel's claim to West Jerusalem, proposed site of an embassy, is unquestioned, and that Palestinians must be disabused of their hope for a capital in Jerusalem. Opponents say a move would undermine the peace process and U.S. credibility in the Islamic world and with Palestinians, and would prejudge the final status of the city. P.L. 104-45, November 8, 1995, provided for the embassy's relocation by May 31, 1999, but granted the President authority, in national security interest, to suspend limitations on State Department expenditures that would be imposed if the embassy did not open. Presidents Clinton and Bush each used the authority several times. The State Department Authorization Act for FY2002-FY2003, P.L. 107-228, September 30, 2002, urged the President to begin relocating the U.S. Embassy "immediately." President Bush replied that the provision would "if construed as mandatory ... impermissibly interfere with the president's constitutional authority to conduct the nation's foreign affairs." The State Department declared, "our view of Jerusalem is unchanged. Jerusalem is a permanent status issue to be negotiated between the parties."

Compliance/Sanctions

President Bush signed the Syria Accountability and Lebanese Sovereignty Restoration Act, P.L. 108-175, on December 12, 2003, to hold Syria accountable for its conduct, including actions that undermine peace. On May 11, 2004, he cited the Act as well as the International Emergency Powers Act, P.L. 95-223, October 28, 1977, as the basis for his authority to issue Executive Order 13399 block property of certain persons and prohibit the exportation or reexportation of certain goods to Syria. In 2006 and 2008, President Bush issued additional executive orders on the subject. On May 7, 2009, President Obama declared a one-year continuance of the national emergency with respect to Syria to allow the sanctions to remain in place. In a letter to Members of Congress, he said, "Syria poses a threat to U.S. interests" and accused its leadership of "supporting terrorist organizations" among other actions.

Israeli Raid on Suspected Syrian Nuclear Site

Sec. 328 of the Conference Report (H.Rept. 110-478) for H.R. 2082, the Intelligence Authorization Act for FY2008, agreed to in the House on December 13, 2007, would have limited spending of the intelligence budget to 30% until each member of the intelligence committees has been informed with respect to intelligence regarding the facility targeted on September 6. The

Administration objected that this provision would circumvent the Executive's authority to control access to extraordinarily sensitive information.[153] The Senate agreed to the Conference Report on February 13, 2008, by a vote of 51-45 and the bill was cleared for the White House, but it was not signed.

On April 24, National Security Advisor Stephen Hadley, CIA Director Michael Hayden, and Director of National Intelligence Mike McConnell presented evidence to congressional committees that the Israeli target was a nuclear reactor, designed by and being built with the assistance of North Korea. Hayden said that the reactor was within weeks or months of completion and, within a year of entering operation, it could have produced enough material for at least one weapon. These officials reportedly acknowledged lack of evidence indicating that Syria was working on nuclear weapons designs and that they had not identified a source of nuclear material for the facility. They expressed "low confidence" that the site was part of a nuclear weapons program.[154] They also denied U.S. involvement in planning or executing the September 6 strike. Experts suggested that the inability to identify a source of fuel raised questions about when the reactor would have been operational and agreed that the inability to identify facilities to separate plutonium from fuel raised further questions about whether the reactor was part of a weapons program.[155] On June 16, International Atomic Energy Agency (IAEA) Director General Mohammed ElBaradei told Al Arabiyah Television, "We have no evidence that Syria has the human resources that would allow it to carry out a large nuclear program. We do not see Syria having nuclear fuel."[156]

Other

S.Res. 10, agreed to by unanimous consent in the Senate on January 8, 2009, and H.Res. 34, agreed to in the House on January 9, by a vote of 390-5, 22 present, recognize Israel's right to defend itself against attacks from Gaza, and reaffirm the United States' strong support for Israel, and support the Israeli-Palestinian peace process.

H.Res. 130, introduced on February 4, 2009, expressing support for the appointment of former Senator George Mitchell as Special Envoy for Middle East Peace.

---

[153] See Statement of Administration Policy regarding H.R. 2082, issued December 11, 2008, http://georgewbush-whitehouse.archives.gov/news/releases/2007/11/20071127-2.html.

[154] Greg Miller, Paul Richter, "U.S. Opens Dossier on Syrian Facility," *Los Angeles Times*, April 25, 2008, "Syrian Reactor Capacity was 1-2 Weapons/Year: CIA, Reuters, April 29, 2008.

[155] Ibid., citing former weapons inspector David Albright.

[156] "Syria Lacks Skills, Fuel for Nuclear Facility: IAEA," Reuters, June 17, 2008.

Figure 1. Israel and Its Neighbors

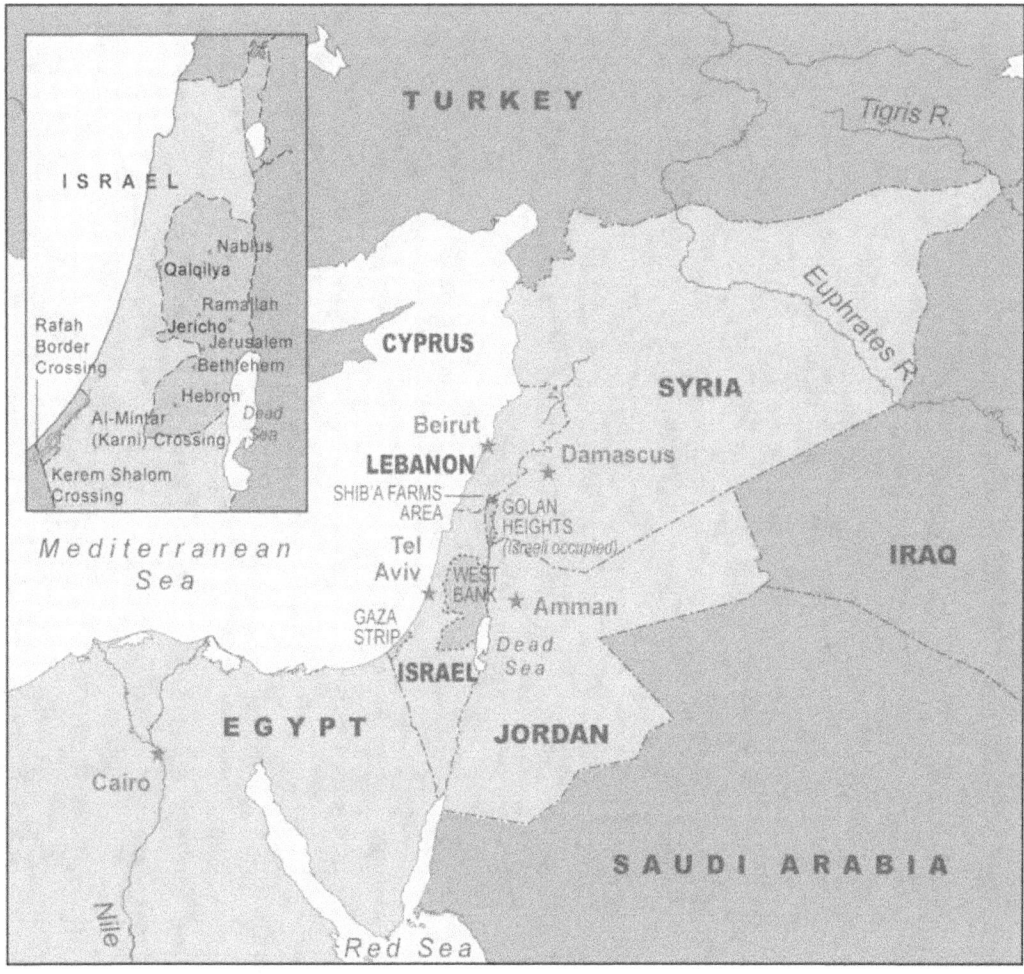

Source: Map Resources. Adapted by CRS.

Author Contact Information

Carol Migdalovitz
Specialist in Middle Eastern Affairs
cmigdalovitz@crs.loc.gov, 7-2667

www.ingramcontent.com/pod-product-compliance
Lightning Source LLC
Chambersburg PA
CBHW080109010626
45794CB00015B/3334